Impossible to Believe

Impossible to Believe

Michael Templeton

IFF
BOOKS

London, UK
Washington, DC, USA

CollectiveInk

First published by iff Books, 2024
iff Books is an imprint of Collective Ink Ltd.,
Unit 11, Shepperton House, 89 Shepperton Road, London, N1 3DF
office@collectiveinkbooks.com
www.collectiveinkbooks.com
www.iff-books.com

For distributor details and how to order please visit the 'Ordering' section on our website.

Text copyright: Michael William Templeton 2023

ISBN: 978 1 80341 633 5
978 1 80341 638 0 (ebook)
Library of Congress Control Number: 2023943699

A CIP catalogue record for this book is available from the British Library.

Design: Lapiz Digital Services

UK: Printed and bound by CPI Group (UK) Ltd, Croydon, CR0 4YY
Printed in North America by CPI GPS partners

We operate a distinctive and ethical publishing philosophy in all areas of our business, from our global network of authors to production and worldwide distribution.

Contents

Introduction

That famous passage cited so often from the preface to *The Order of Things* by Foucault takes on a different meaning in our time. Foucault famously used the quotation from Borges as a dramatic example of a system of taxonomy that gives an order to things that otherwise cannot be ordered. Foucault explains that this moment in the text moved him "to laughter that shattered ... all the familiar landmarks of my thought—*our* thought that bears the stamp of our age."[1] The point of this fantastic example is to demonstrate how "another system" of thought reveals "the limitation of our own, the impossibility of thinking *that*."[2] Foucault's example works because reading this system against our own system of logic, reason, scientific method and truth, of common sense, even—that the system that forms the Chinese encyclopedia is clearly fantastic and unthinkable. This example from the realms of the fabulous is meant to serve as a springboard from which Foucault will draw out his project of tracing the archaeology of order and meaning up into our own time. Of course, we must understand at every step along the way that the absurd example from the preface will never serve to offer us a point from which we can look around our own enlightened times and think, at least we no longer think that. In any case, Foucault's method and system does follow a careful order and logic. There is a method and there are clear objects of study even if Foucault does endlessly remove the very possibility of fixed objects and transcendent methods.

Toward the end of the book, as we are led toward the ascendency of the contemporary world after the Classical age, we must follow a series of propositions and shifts in thought which undermine language in relation to thought. I have no intention of entering into a critique or analysis of Foucault or *The Order of Things*. Rather, what we should consider is an example

1

from Foucault's text that serves as a point of departure as we consider the function of language and thought in the twenty-first century. In turning to "man" as an object of knowledge, Foucault explains:

> When natural history becomes biology, when the analysis of wealth becomes economics, when, above all, reflection on language becomes philology, and Classical *discourse*, in which being and representation found their common locus, is eclipsed, then, in the profound upheaval of such an archaeological mutation, man appears in his ambiguous position as an object of knowledge, and as a subject that knows; enslaved sovereign, observed spectator.[3]

This opening in knowledge and being that comes with the emergence of language and the emergence of the historical "man," this is the lynchpin from which we move into the episteme of the contemporary world. Yet, in looking around at what people claim to know, at the actions and beliefs of individuals in the contemporary world, and the systems of verification from which we are able to arrive at something that can be understood as true—looking at the most common features of everyday life, it becomes inevitable that we look at Foucault's order of things and wonder at "the impossibility of thinking *that*." How could anyone think what Foucault describes and how could anyone believe anything they believe at all?

Unlike the old peasantry in which natural ignorance was a function of an isolated world, the new peasantry is conditioned to their ignorance by a cultural logic which denies anything exterior to consumer culture. In this dream world of consumerism sustained within a digital heaven, or "metaverse" as if the universe within which everything exists were insufficient, knowledge and belief have been taken over by something that escapes the order of things.

Natural ignorance has given way to the organized spectacle of error. The "new towns" [subdivisions] of technological pseudo-peasantry are the clearest indications, inscribed on the land, of the break with historical time on which they are founded: their motto might well be: "On this spot nothing will ever happen—and *nothing ever has*."[4]

An organized spectacle of error is the inevitable result of a population who derive all knowledge of the world from within the spectacle. Debord's theory in which the mediation of the image has been fractalized and injected into the most intimate spheres of everyday life. Our very DNA operates as an image of ourselves through the commodification of genetic information by things like *Ancestry.com* in which we can all find our authentic selves. What could be more authentic that our DNA? And we can now publicize our authentic genetic selves with social media. We can even put our own images of our DNA at the head of a Google search with a simple Search Engine Optimization. We are always already a public image of ourselves, and we are all what the Invisible Committee (an anonymous group of French political writers) called the Young-Girl—even if we resist it by trying to hide. The machines are at work rendering us in digital form and transforming us into data points that can be analyzed and optimized.

I will say more about the Young-Girl in a later chapter. At this stage it is enough to explain that the Young-Girl is "the beacon-commodity of the fifth industrial revolution which enables the sale of all the others, from life insurance to nuclear power, the monstrous and very real dream of the most intrepid, the most fantastical of retailers: autonomous commodities that walk, talk, and silence, *the thing that is finally alive*, that no longer seizes life, but digests it."[5] The Young-Girl is the living being that consumes and is consumed by itself and for all.

One could argue that the Young-Girl finds its ultimate expression in someone like Donald Trump—a man who does not exist beyond his image. The facts of Donald Trump and his life are well-known. He has made a brand purely on the basis of being wealthy. Trump's brand is wealth and opulence. Well before he became a reality TV personality, he was already a celebrity who was famous for high-end hotels and luxury living that are all completely beyond the average middle-class American. With his rise as a reality TV celebrity, he managed to carve out the fiction that he is a shrewd and potentially ruthless businessman—the kind of business boss who built America with his gut instincts for talent and success. None of this holds up to even the most casual scrutiny. The myth of the great men of business who built America does not include multiple bankruptcies, for example. And none of these things are features of middle-class life. That middle-class Americans have come to admire such "virtue" is a foregone conclusion, but none of these traits would suggest that Trump is one of us, one of the people, as it were. What people identify with, what gets Trump the ceremonial seat at America's middle-class table is not his talents. It is not his success as a businessman. Nor is it his success on television. What makes Trump a man of the people is his brand of populism that renders him an object of both identification and exchange. Trump is perfectly willing to say absolutely anything. Indeed, it seems apparent that he cannot help himself from saying whatever pops into his head no matter how ridiculous or insane. Trump has also been perfectly happy to align himself with what we now refer to as "white grievance," the idea that white people can lay claim to the same forms of oppression, marginalization, and victimhood as every other subject position. Still, all of this kind of posturing would have failed not long ago. What has changed is the way individuals and groups access and process this kind of performance and language. White grievance can gain traction, and the absurd equivocating that characterizes white grievance can succeed only when the cultural conditions make it possible for individuals to find an equivalency between themselves and the exchange of ideas that render both ideas and subjects as exchangeable commodities. White grievance is equal in value to any other form of oppression simply because oppression of any kind is one commodity among all others.

The rise of white grievance, and with it the theory that white people will be replaced by non-white people and immigrants, has its origins in the rise of the Civil Rights movement. Alexander Hinton explains that the belief that white people are victims of a so-called "White genocide" has a long history: "While the idea of White genocide dates back to the Nazis, eugenics, and beyond, the term was coined after the Civil Rights movement, which destabilized the long-standing U.S. White power patriarchal order. White power discourses began to be reframed in terms of victimization and grievance."[6] Trump tapped into this narrative as part of his brand. By framing his own brand—and I choose this term deliberately—within an existing one, Trump was able to offer middle-class white people, not just those at the margins of society, a commodity they could easily buy that confirmed their fears of the other. The persistent fear that urban crime, for example, something that has been historically linked to black people, would somehow come to their safe affluent neighborhoods was given a consumable form once it became part of the shrewd businessman brand that is Trump—the celebrity Young-Girl in excelsis.

We should return to the point where Debord describes the status of a celebrity as a spectacular approximation of a living human:

The individual who in the service of the spectacle is placed in stardom's spotlight is in fact the opposite of an individual, and as clearly the enemy of the individual in himself as of the individual in others. In entering the spectacle as a model to be identified with, he renounces all autonomy in order to be identified with the general law of obedience to the course of things.[7]

The public figure who identifies most efficiently with the general course of things will necessarily emerge as the political figure who speaks the language of the people. It is at this stage that we can speak of a figure such as Donald Trump who can be easily described in the same terms the Invisible Committee used to describe Silvio Berlusconi. In observing what they call "the shipwreck of the state," the wreckage of the modern nation-state after it has been cannibalized by contemporary semiocapital, what we see in a figure like Trump "isn't a single individual who has taken power but a form-of-life: that narrow-minded, self-seeking, philofascist petty-entrepreneur."[8] Instead of a philofascist, we have a trustafarian real estate fraud, but the essence of the form-of-life remains the same. Still further, Trump attempts to cast his brand as one that is "based on business as the only form of socialization after the family—and he who embodies it *represents* no one and certainly not a majority, but *is* a perfectly discernible form-of-life with which only a small fraction of the population can identify."[9] But Trump is really little more than "the clone of the neighborhood asshole."[10] The distinction here is the "form-of-life." Trump is not to be understood as a singular individual who somehow has the capacity to harness the powers of the spectacle and global capital to attain and wield power. Rather, it is a form of a type of person, a model of a way of being, that is invested into a figure like Donald Trump through the mediating power of the spectacle as it is exponentially advanced within the world of cyber-culture. Trump is no more a "man" than any of the childish figures trotted out in spectacular sites like professional wrestling. It is in this way that Trump can embody and enact the spectacular false differences that exist among individuals. Rather, we now have a population who are living under a system of homogeneity unlike any that has ever existed. The perception of difference must be manufactured along lines that are utterly facile but deeply entrenched. Thus we have witnessed a resurgence of things like white supremacists and ultra-nationalists who can prey on facile and childish fears.

Trump's ability to embody the neighborhood asshole works in his favor as millions of neighborhood assholes find validation in his ignorance, petty resentments, and hatred of anyone who is different from the stereotypical white suburban type that actually does in fact dominate middle-class American life. The neighborhood asshole is the brand that sells, and this commodity precedes Donald Trump. Most significant to all of this is the fact that Trump is a clownish buffoon, and I will argue that it is clownish buffoonery that is the key to understanding the success of Trump and others like him. Clownish buffoonery, or histrionic displays, are symptoms of a world in which everyday life must be rendered in the form of a public performance. Not just any performance, but a grotesque spectacle which outstrips any notion of performativity in the sense that Judith Butler has theorized, in which modes of power deploy "discursively and performatively instituted modes of temporality that are invoked within the terms of a normative framework."[11] These performances are more on the order of the geek show in which the lowest of the freaks, usually a person debased by poverty, tortures and kills a live chicken by biting its head off. None of these grotesque spectacles alter reality. They are spectacular performances designed to evoke the same abject impulses that once invigorated the crowds at carnival sideshows where they could gaze at reflections of their own sickening fantasies of themselves.

While religious faith has moved into the arena of theater and amusement parks and ideological belief has been stripped of the materiality of lived life, the role of public figures and political leaders is now the province of sideshow spectacles. Public life and political discourse have more in common with freak shows and circus geeks, and this has everything to do with the loss of the consistency of belief which is replaced by spectacular forms of belief which operate as mediating processes between vacuous individuality and the spectacle that has been rocketed by the speed of cyberculture and semiocapital.

Douglas Kellner draws on the spectacle directly to characterize the nightmare that is Donald Trump. Kellner explains that Trump's very existence depends entirely on a society that is completely overwritten by the society of the spectacle and the "success" of Trump is completely a function of spectacular culture: "Trump is ... the first major U.S. presidential candidate to pursue politics as entertainment and thus to collapse the distinction between entertainment, news, and politics, greatly expanding the domain of spectacle theorized by Debord."[12] Elsewhere Kellner concedes that Trump is "a cauldron of resentment," and for this reason he is capable of tapping into a feeling of resentment that pervades American life—feelings of resentment that are well-founded insofar as markers of the quality of life have consistently diminished over the past half century for most people, and large numbers of people have many good reasons to resent the sources of power and authority in the United States. Nonetheless, whipping this resentment into a pseudo-messianic cult of personality can only happen on the scale that it has within a mode of life and within an ideological moment that make it possible for a billionaire and an imbecile like Trump to emerge as the savior of the common people. Kellner is correct to attribute the rise of Trump and the entire apparatus of delusions that attend him to a spectacular mode of understanding the world and everything in it.

The election of Barak Obama to the Presidency was a crisis point for racist America. With the election of a black man to the highest office in the land, a rupture occurred in the collective imagination of much of the nation. Even the most latent of racists witnessed the unthinkable moment when a black man took control of what they like to view as the greatest nation on Earth. This was horrifying to them, and the kinds of things said of Obama reflected this fear and horror.

No matter one's opinion of Obama's politics, the kinds of things that were focused on him had nothing to do with politics and everything to do with racist fear. The most vitriolic and the loudest attacks on Obama came in the form of the so-called birther movement. The idea that Obama was not legitimately eligible to be President because he was foreign born is a thin smokescreen for the fact that the claim was not simply that he was born in a foreign country, but that he was born in an African country. Obama, they claimed, was not just a black man who supplanted a role that legitimately belongs to white men, he was an African and therefore blacker than an American black man. None of these attacks has any merit or foundation, and they were fomented by the likes of Donald Trump long before he ever ran for President. The bottom line is that the election of Barak Obama presented a crisis for American whiteness and the status quo that comes with it—the firm belief that when we say "American" we are talking about a white heterosexual male.

Coming on the heels of this, the Supreme Court ruled in 2015 that the Fourteenth Amendment applied to non-heterosexual people and allowed for the legal rights of gay people to be married. Yet another critical piece of the white heterosexual edifice began to crumble and this one presented a real monstrosity in the eyes of many people. A society so deeply heteronormative was confronted with the *legal* fact that they could no longer relegate non-hetero people to a strictly marginal position in the hierarchy of American life.

As if this were not enough, in 2014 President Obama signed legislation which added gender identity to the list of categories protected against discrimination in the workplace. This opened the door to protections for transgender and all non-binary sexualities, and this rendered non-binary individuals as yet another force to be reckoned with in daily life, yet another "monstrosity" that homophobic and racist people could no longer simply relegate to marginality.

These are three of the most prominent moments in the cultural life of the United States that galvanized many into a body of voters who would rally around Trump. Crucial to this message and those who were empowered by it is that these events help Trump create the myth that ordinary white heterosexual and middle-class people have become an oppressed minority that needed to stop the march of monstrous "others" who would replace them and create a nation guided by sexual deviance and the atavistic impulses of black Africans. Trump capitalized on these ignorant fears and stoked them into a movement founded on the oldest and most virulent racist and bigoted ideals, and his willingness to behave in the most childish ways served as proof that he would do anything to speak up for the now marginalized white Christian majority.

As millions of middle-class Americans have seen their lives devalued by the systems of control that render them commodities that derive their full value as units of exchange while holding out the promise of freedom that can only come in the form of an endless freedom to shop and dine, the political landscape of American life shifted to expose not the threat of an imagined other, but the poverty of everyday life, this same swarm of people were offered an image-machine that would give vent to their most base desires in the forms of sick fantasies of being the minority that is under threat. The bigoted fears that could be assuaged with economic padding had eroded, and these fears flooded forth in a torrent. Trump was there to give voice to these fears and virulent hatreds. Stoked within terrariums of algorithmically refined pseudo-information and ratified by the economic validity offered by the debt relation, the American swarm was poised to accept anything that adhered to a set of delusions that already functioned as facts. So it was when Hillary Clinton referred to Trump's supporters as "deplorables," they were only too happy to wallow in the epithet. White grievance and things like the imaginary war on Christianity had already disposed millions of people to see themselves as outsiders in a world overrun by sexual deviants, atavistic minorities and foreigners, and anti-Christian political extremists. In a world overrun by freaks, the white, middle-class majority could now see themselves as the freaks. The fact is, the average middle-class white American has been fully ameliorated to their role as the hyper-domesticated and infantilized Young-Girl. Their ferocity is the expression of their impotence.

It is a popular sentiment to see Trump as a fascist demagogue, that he has modeled himself after fascist dictators both historical and current. It is certainly true that Trump tried in every way to consolidate his power as President into a singular force that he alone would wield with absolute caprice. Yet, there are other factors at work in the contemporary world that would undermine Trump's own desire and the desires of those who enabled him. Panayota Gounari lays out some of the key features of the contemporary fascist demagogue. Drawing on a wide field of research, Gounari offers a clear code for how to recognize the authoritarian leader/demagogue and it is clear that Donald Trump fits the bill in every way. The fourth point is curious, and I quote it in its entirety:

The emergence of the authoritarian leader, who relies on personal politics as an individual brand, what Ruth Wodak calls "personalization and commodification of current politics and politicians." These "leaders employ front stage performance techniques that are linked to popular celebrity culture" (Wodak 2015, 21). Trump, further, embodies many characteristics of the "authoritarian personality," (Adorno et al., 1950); power and "toughness" are promoted as virtues while the binaries "dominance–submission", "strong-weak", "leader-follower" are central in his persona and discourse. There is an overemphasis on the conventionalized attributes of the ego and an exaggerated assertion of strength and toughness. Despite all of the leader's material and symbolic power he still uses a narrative of victimhood for himself (as is, for instance, the case with Trump's treatment of the press). Finally, he demonstrates "destructiveness and cynicism" manifested as generalized hostility and vilification of humans.[13]

I do not take issue with any of this, however, I will draw attention to one feature which Gounari passes over as if it is not of greater significance. The fact that Trump is one "who relies on personal politics as an individual brand" is far more important than the above definition would allow. It is Trump's brand that is in fact the most important feature in all of this, and the fact that the man, Donald Trump, is indistinguishable from his brand is central to how the entire political machine functions. This feature of the brand as politics goes far beyond Trump, although his is clearly the most obvious example. What we see in the Trump brand is the reification of the vectors of semiocapital into an image-machine that transforms the political into a carnival of the spectacle.

Trump isn't a person or an actor; he is a freak, a sickening projection of the worst features of American life as they are enacted on television and the Internet for people to gaze upon their own fantasy projections of all that they fear and revile. Trump is the Young-Girl in all her grotesque bloom. The success of Trump has more to do with his willingness to bite the head off the live chicken than with any complex account of demagoguery and totalitarianism. He embodies the extreme of spectacular performances of belief in a world in which the foundation for genuine belief has been completely eroded and been thoroughly replaced with the most flimsy and histrionic performances of life and belief.

Like many others, I watched the run-up to the 2016 Presidential election with a mix of amusement and horror. Listening to the news on the radio, I heard one adult after another make claims that were utterly preposterous. Ben Carson's infamous account of the Egyptian pyramids as storage containers for grain stands out, but it is only one of the most obvious and silly examples. Like many others, I made the fatal error of assuming there simply were not enough people in the United States stupid enough or deluded enough to believe this nonsense. Then Donald Trump ascended to the Presidency. We know what happened after that.

The mistake I made, and I believe many still make, was to relegate the mass support for blitheringly ignorant ideas as a symptom of stupidity. The facts are more complicated than this, and what I eventually came to understand was that few people actually believed any of the nonsense spewed by politicians of any stripe, and that a vast number of people are operating under an entirely different set of conditions than what can properly be called belief.

Against this backdrop in which knowledge and belief are no longer bound by anything other than the thin air of the digital image and forms of power are expressed through forms of life that are assembled from pure histrionics, this book will examine the ways individuals are situated within systems of control that offer an illusion of freedom through an exchange of autonomy in the form of the debt relation. Under current conditions of global financial capital, individuals are free to the extent that they "behave" in accordance with an economic paradigm that denies the very possibility of freedom. The illusion of freedom and autonomy is gained through access to digital expressions of the self which are spectacular self-images which stand in for active beings. We are pacified and passive in the extreme, yet our digital image operates within the exchange of images as if it were an avatar of a free subject.

These conditions carry into the cultural space once occupied by religion and faith. Amid the histrionic demonstrations of profound faith, what emerges is the total absence of faith. In its place are faith-based amusement park and shopping mall pseudo churches which provide faith in the same forms as service station hotdogs and taquitos. The perception of a war on Christianity masks the reality of a world in which faith is utterly meaningless. The abject fear that there is nothing to replace this faith produces the terrified rage of a population devoid of the ground on which faith once functioned.

As a result, individuals cling to bold but histrionic demonstrations of beliefs they cannot support because there is nothing to replace them. What follows is an attempt to understand what we are living with as the conditions for belief in anything at all are lost, and we are no longer individuals but atomized units of exchange that find the full measure of their validity in the image generated by credit scores and purchasing power.

Notes

1. Foucault, Michel. *The Order of Things*. xv.
2. Foucault, Michel. *The Order of Things*. xv.
3. Foucault, Michel. *The Order of Things*. 312.
4. Debord, Guy. *The Society of the Spectacle*. 312.
5. Tiqqun. *Preliminary Materials for a Theory of the Young-Girl*. 138–139.
6. Hinton, Alexander. *It Can Happen Here*. 63.
7. Debord. *The Society of the Spectacle*. 39.
8. Tiqqun. *This is Not a Program*. 99.
9. Tiqqun. *This is Not a Program*. 99.
10. Tiqqun. *This is Not a Program*. 99.
11. Butler, Judith. *Gender Trouble*. 29.
12. Kellner, Douglas. *The Politics of the Spectacle*. 6.
13. Gounari, Panayota. "Authoritarianism, Discourse and Social Media: Trump as the 'American Agitator.'" 211.

Doing Your Part with the
Aspiration Credit Card

Everything that begins as comedy ends as a dirge in the void.
Bolano. *The Savage Detectives*, 468

*Everything that begins as comedy ends as a comic monologue, but
we aren't laughing anymore.*
Bolano. *The Savage Detectives*, 469

The World Resources Institute reports that more than 70% of
the greenhouse gases emitted in the world are from energy
sector industries: "(O)nly 100 investor and state-owned fossil
fuel companies are responsible for around 70 percent of the
world's historical GHG emissions."[1] These are enormous
public and private enterprises that are the primary engines
of global climate change. Nevertheless, the responsibility for
greenhouse gas emissions is placed on the individual consumer
who has little to no control over the overwhelming mass of the
greenhouse gas emissions that are fueling a global catastrophe.
The great trick of global Empire is to divert responsibility for
the devastation of global climate change onto the victims of
global climate change. In fact, the only real drive to combat
global climate change has been to create the illusion that the
individual can alter their lifestyles and consumer choices
toward a beneficent way of living that will reduce carbon
emissions enough to stop what amounts to a catastrophe of
global proportions. This is, of course, central to the neoliberal
mode of thought which centers everything on unrestrained
global market capitalism and the drive to privatize virtually
all sectors of life. The central mystification within this mode of
thinking is that one is responsible for one's world as a private
and free citizen, and citizenship is defined by one's status as a

15

consumer. Consumer choice is the free democratic choice par excellence. One is a citizen of a free society by being a free consumer, and the problem of global climate change is up to the free consumer.

There is no end to the products we can buy that claim to reduce our individual "carbon footprint" (I cannot imagine a more quaint term for the wholesale destruction of life on the planet). Even national programs to foster a sense of common duty toward the reduction of greenhouse gas emissions seem desperately naïve. The UK, for instance, adopted its "Low-Carbon Transition Plan" with the basic assumption that the key to transforming the use of greenhouse gases lies with a change in consumer behavior. But, as Jeanette Webb points out: "The citizen consumer, taught to equate freedom and self-worth with individual rights to consumption of an unending variety of positional goods, while being made individually responsible for life risks, is encouraged to regard the common good as a burdensome cost."[2] These kinds of governmental and civic drives to change individual behavior fail for at least two reasons: Consumers do not change their behavior as consumers because to consume is to be free. One cannot be a member of society without consuming goods, and the production, transportation, support, etc. of and for these goods are precisely what drives global climate change. Second, consumers do not change as long as producers continue to funnel them consumer products no matter the consequences of the production of these products. We may also add an additional reason which is that many people know that the real cause of global climate change is large private and governmental operations which produce the vast majority of greenhouse gases, and these same people know they are utterly powerless in the face of this fact.

It is in the conclusions that Webb points toward the complexity of the problem of laying the responsibility for global climate change at the feet of the consumer. The idea that the consumer and the individual can make sufficient changes to alter the course of global climate change is circumvented by the very nature of neoliberal ideology. Webb explains in the conclusion: "In adopting an individualized consumer model of citizenship, government strategy simultaneously obscures or marginalizes societal analyses, and obstructs acknowledgement of the contradictions between the neo-liberal political economy and sustainable society."[3] Webb's is a sociological study, but it opens the field for further analysis by pointing to the contradictions inherent in the "neo-liberal political economy." This type of approach necessarily obscures its efforts to make substantive changes as it transforms the problem itself into the solution. The strategy of global consumer capital is to mediate the problem of global climate change with the *market itself* by providing a nearly infinite array of choices of consumer goods alleged to help combat the causes of climate change. The consumer-citizen needs only to begin spending their money on products that offer goods and services that purport to act toward ameliorating the crisis of global climate change. This type of maneuver is central to the society of the spectacle in which the consumer-citizen finds its full measure of value in relation to the forms and types of consumption available to them. The conditions Webb begins to describe, and the conditions within which individuals come to believe that they are both responsible for and able to mitigate a global catastrophe, begin to come about at the "historical moment at which the commodity completes its colonization of social life. It is not just that the relationship to commodities is now plain to see — commodities are *all* there is to see; the world we see is the world of the commodity."[4] A global matrix that defines citizenship, indeed, it defines subjectivity itself which I will address below, as a consumer creates a mode of existence in which social life is determined by the presence and acquisition of commodities. One participates in life itself by operating as a consumer. Global capital is able to provide images of a solution to global climate change simply by presenting a set of free choices for consumers in the form of commodities that claim to ameliorate the problem of greenhouse gases and global climate change. There is more to be said about this, but an example for what I have described thus far will open these issues much wider.

The Aspiration credit/debit card, part of Aspiration Financial, LLC, promises to plant a certain number of trees that correspond to the amount of money you spend using the Aspiration card. The network of banks that are tied into the Aspiration card also allow you, under specific conditions, to link your existing credit or debit card to the Aspiration program. Simply by spending money with your Aspiration credit card, you can participate in a tree planting program that claims to combat the greenhouse gases which are the cause of global climate change. With the mere act of buying things, by enacting your role as a consumer, you can do your part in combatting global climate change. The Aspiration card is ideal since it allows consumers to buy virtually anything and still do their part in fighting global climate change. The freedom of the consumer-citizen is advanced as the fight against global catastrophe is equally advanced. The name of the credit card alone tropes heavily on green politics. Aspiration is to breathe. When we use our Aspiration credit card, we are not just spending money, we are breathing the clean air we have done our part to create. We are also breathing the sigh of relief that comes with participating in a program that claims to fight global climate change.

This type of non-action is called interpassivity, and it may be the apotheosis of spectacular life in which non-action and literal passivity are experienced as action and activism. Zizek offers a theory of interpassivity in which "it is the object itself that 'enjoys the show' instead of me [or anyone]" ("The Interpassive Subject"). Interpassivity is the condition in which one is able to take part in an electronic representation of events via an electronic mode of interactivity as a passive participant. Robert Pfaller explains further as he sums up Zizek by explaining that in interpassivity, "the allegedly 'subjective,' 'interior' entities such as feelings, emotions, thoughts, convictions etc. can have an 'objective,' 'exterior' existence."[5] The laugh track is Zizek's example, but this seems quaint in the era of social media in which one is able to allow a simple hashtag to operate as the fetish-sign which stands in for one's deepest inner convictions. The modes of digital interactive engagement made possible by social media allow one to engage events through a simulated proxy. In fact, they force us to engage by proxy as passive consumers of events rather than active participants in events.[6] One need not actually do anything at all, least of all make any substantive changes in one's lifestyle, to do one's part to save the earth. A person with a high enough line of credit could buy the parts and tools necessary to alter their truck so that it burns excess oil and gas and belches massive smoke to protest the environmentalist ideals that hope to actually do something about global climate change. The system has made it possible to do your part while working directly against the very things it promises to do. In any case, "doing your part" is a pure illusion, or delusion as the case may be. We do not need to question the claim that the financial giant behind the Aspiration card does in fact plant trees. What we can question is whether or not planting these trees amounts to anything when the global capitalist machine that drives climate change is not only unchanged but actually strengthened by using a credit card. In fact, it is the system of global finance capitalism that creates and sustains the division between the sources of power and destruction and virtually everyone else, and the Aspiration credit card is most active in sustaining financial capital than anything else. It must be, or it would not exist.

We do not need to dig deep to see what the Aspiration card is. The terms and conditions clearly state that "Aspiration is

Make Earth Green Again, LLC ... a limited liability company. An affiliate, Aspiration Financial." Again, there is no reason to doubt the promise that they are planting trees in accordance with their claims. This is also stated within the terms and conditions. Most crucial is the fact that this credit card and the financial institution that issues it stand out as exemplary of the kinds of interpassive choices that mystify the realities of deferring action on climate change to a simple cause and effect relationship between consumer choice and material action with regard to very real issues. We could choose any number of examples. The Aspiration card stands out because this offer and this promise open up a much wider set of problems than the simple interpassive maneuver of posting memes, for example, to ally oneself with a social or political issue. The Aspiration card is emblematic of a number of things: it operates as a platform for an entirely interpassive form of participation in solving the problem of a global catastrophe while diverting attention from the problem itself. This program also creates a pathway by which one can operate as a global citizen in the role of a global consumer. It also works as a conduit by which one enters into the system of financial capital which is the engine of global capital. The beneficiaries of this last maneuver are the financial institutions who own the debt. The Aspiration card and the program of planting trees based on individual spending facilitate the solitary and singular point of access to the society of the spectacle, citizen activism on a global scale, and a personal role in the system of financial capital that subjectivizes the individual who is fundamentally captured by this system. Consumer, producer, and citizen are condensed into the same entity with the elementary operations of a smart phone.

Homo Consumptor
The emergence of the bourgeois subject theorized by Habermas depended on "the public engaged in rational-critical debate

(freedom of opinion and speech, freedom of press, freedom of assembly and association, etc.) and the political function of private people in this public sphere (right of petition, equality of vote, etc.)."[7] Something like rational-critical debate necessarily demands that individuals engage the world on a level that is perceived as real, and that these same individuals are able to engage other individuals on the level of an accepted understanding of what is real. That what is taken as real is contingent is a given. What is at issue is that the emergence and function of citizen-subjects depends on this mutual acceptance of reality. To this, we may add Foucault's analysis of the economic subject which emerges at roughly the same historical moment as Homo economicus: economic man. For Foucault, the citizen-subject exists as a subject of the economic system to the extent that civil society is the global form of the economic system in which citizen-subjects recognize themselves, each other, and the reality within which they must exist. As Foucault explains, "homo economicus" begins to function under a specific mode of neoliberal economics when this economic system can take as given that subjects respond in systematic ways to environmental variables.[8] What we must understand is that citizen-subjects operate and engage in rational-critical debate based on their individual responses to environmental variables taken as real, and from within these elemental conditions a form of civil society can emerge and function at least at a minimal level. These elemental conditions are abstracted and disengaged from accepted realities as we move into the society of the spectacle. Debord's insight is that spectacular culture does not entail engagement with real environmental conditions. It is entirely derived from images which mediate real environmental conditions and are then consumed in place of real environmental conditions. This is what Debord refers to as "society's real unreality"; it is the unreality understood as real and consumed as real.[9] The most fundamental conditions of the bourgeois public sphere and that form of citizen-subject called Homo economicus are now operating not within a public sphere, but within a formal abstraction that negates and takes the place of the public sphere. Rather than something like Habermas's rational-critical debate, we are now operating as economic units, atomized economic producers and consumers of a vast collection of images which stand in for real environmental conditions. As Foucault states: "(S)ociety appears as the producer of conforming behavior with which it is satisfied in return for a certain investment."[10] Citizen-subjects are homogenized and conditioned to understand their role as citizens within the terms of consumerism. We are free to the extent that we freely consume, and the exercise of our fundamental right to free consumption is the mark of a free citizen. All of this unfolds in an utterly unreal and abstract network of exchange. When we add the contemporary dimensions of financial capital and digital exchange, we enter into a realm fully divorced from real environmental conditions and supplanted with conditions that are fabricated as strategies of consumerism.

Another way of looking at this is that the modern nation-state emerges simultaneously with the homogenization of diverse populations into something that can be understood as "the people." The people of the United States function as a single entity even if, perhaps especially if, the people are in fact a loose collection of vastly different individuals. To achieve this, the modern nation-state required that the people appear as the origin of the nation. What is in reality a heterogeneous population can appear to themselves as a singular entity only at that point in which they, the people, recognize themselves as the source of sovereignty and power. The passage to the people necessarily means there is a tendency "toward identity and homogeneity internally while posing its difference from and excluding what remains outside."[11] The second, but equally important, step in the emergence of the people is "the eclipse of internal differences through the *representation* of the whole population by a hegemonic group, race, class, etc."[12] Hardt and Negri's point in outlining this process is to demonstrate that we have moved away from the dominance and sovereignty of the nation-state into the age of Empire in which a global system of economic relations outstrips the nation-state and the people even as both nation-state and the people still operate as if they take precedence. One of the ways the mystification of the stability of the people remains in place is the insertion into the public consciousness of a spectacular simulacrum of the ideals, systems, and beliefs of the people. No matter how utterly fictional these ideals, beliefs, and systems may have been, there was a stable hegemonic investment in the existence of these things. As we move into the twenty-first century, these ideals, beliefs, and systems are taken over by a system of images of images.

The people and the public sphere in which they derived their sense of being was predicated on an outside and an inside. The people were understood as the public side of individual existence while the private realm of everyday life was a separate sphere. As Hardt and Negri explain, "the outside is the place proper to politics, where the action of the individual is exposed in the presence of others and there seeks recognition."[13] This is critical to understanding how something like the Aspiration card insinuates itself into the public imagination and takes the place of the outside in which individuals expose themselves and interact as citizen-subjects engaged in rational critical debate. With the society of the spectacle, all individual engagement is mediated by images of public engagement. Rather than a physical space of the outside, we have the digital, cyberspace of abstract mediation in which individual action is performed by proxy. What we have is a "virtual place, or more accurately, a *non-place* of politics."[14] Individual action is mediated within this non-place of the spectacle which is "at once unified and diffuse in such a way that it is impossible to distinguish any outside from inside—the natural from the social."[15] Thus, the outside and inside are expunged along with any substantial form of rational critical debate and the citizen-subject becomes indistinguishable from the consumer. Nothing is left of the "real" from which individuals form a sense of the world where they live and the ideas they act upon: "The spectacle destroys any collective form of sociality—individualizing social actors in their separate automobiles and in front of separate video screens—and at the same time imposes a new mass sociality, a new uniformity of action and thought."[16] With the Aspiration card, individuals perform acts of global citizenship with the notion that they are combatting global climate change, and they perform this as a diffuse mass individually and separately. The non-action of using a credit card stands in for real actions that can no longer take place since the outside in which private individuals engage each other as citizen-subjects in rational critical debate has been nullified by the spectacular non-space of the digital realm. The pathways by which thought and action are abstracted from lived life and through the non-space of the digital realm toward a complete re-configuration of Homo economicus into something entirely other.

The example of the Aspiration card performs something akin to condensation and displacement. The promise of the Aspiration card with regard to individual actions toward combatting climate change displaces an entire set of civic actions and conditions. These include things such as civil engagement among living bodies, the acceptable conditions of good citizenship, the very act of planting trees, ecological commitments, the entire liberal/left ideology of social responsibility, and ultimately the self-satisfaction of doing something good. This same transaction displaces the passive nature of allowing a mode of consumption to stand in for a real and tangible action. It displaces the fact that individuals have little to no impact on the global catastrophe of climate change. Condensation and displacement work to divert the citizen-subject toward their role as consumer-citizen. One is no longer simply Homo economicus. Under this regime of economic and social (in)action, we become Homo consumptor. And as Homo consumptor of the twenty-first century, we are not only captured within the society of the spectacle, we are increasingly compelled to communicate in terms that are not human.

The forms of communication which make consumer capital operate are now totally defined by the digital realm. Digital communication is in every way different than the ways in which living humans communicate, and these digital mechanisms in fact deny humanity in order to function at all. Contemporary consumer commerce is conducted online. While Debord's vision of the spectacle depended on a central site of mediation between the world of images and individuals who interact with the image, the contemporary digital realm has made it possible for spectacular culture to colonize the deepest reaches of the human psyche. The spectacle claims us on the Internet which adds exponential degrees of alienation, separation, and isolation. A consumer is most likely to use their Aspiration card online, and all of the economic processes enacted by the Aspiration card unfold in the digital realm. In applying these transactions to Homo consumptor, we need to understand the modes of communication which define every element of the entire transactional process. The modes of communication that define contemporary exchange underpin the forms of subjectivity that define Homo consumptor. Where we see a divergence from a citizen-subject who understands itself in relation to real environmental conditions toward a citizen-subject who is conditioned entirely by spectacular conditions, we can add a citizen-subject who is forced to communicate along channels that are fundamentally inhuman. Human communication, the ways living humans exchange information and arrive at understanding (or even conflict for that matter), is ultimately restricted by basic human cognitive capacities. Living human communication unfolds as conjunction, in Bifo's terms, and this type of communication is a function of living cognitive capacities: "Conjunction is the meeting and fusion of rounded and irregular forms that infuse in a manner that is imprecise, unrepeatable, imperfect, and continuous."[17] It should be immediately apparent that this type of communication is useless to global capital. It is not commodifiable simply because that which is unrepeatable is not reproducible as an interchangeable commodity. The form of digital communication that defines global capital must be endlessly accessible to digital exchange. This requires defined bits of information that can be processed and digitally comprehended for use as units of exchange. This is what Bifo defines as connection: "Rather than a fusion of segments. Connection entails a simple effect of machinic functionality. In order to connect, segments must be compatible and open to interfacing and interoperability. Connection requires these segments to be linguistically compatible."[18] In the connective mode of communication, living human desires, needs, feelings, senses, and even awareness are transformed into usable bits of digital data points which can be accessed, used and exchanged. In other words, living human experience is condensed into digital signifiers which stand in for life. Bifo says as much when he explains that "the digital web spreads and expands by progressively *reducing* more and more elements to a format, a standard and a code that make different segments compatible."[19] The digital mode of exchange "reduces" or condenses living human communication to standardized signifiers that can be exchanged.

As we consider the citizen-subject under this regime of communication, what we find is that the living human that occupies the role of citizen and subject is increasingly deformed. As digital connective communication supersedes human conjunction, we lose touch with the very faculties which make it possible to make contact with the environmental conditions which are the basis of the real. We also lose contact with the living capacity to communicate with each other. The dominance of connectivity "generates pathologies in the psychic sphere and in social relations."[20] These pathologies emerge as a living human finds its only mode of understanding foreclosed by the artificial life-world in which it is forced to exist. Thus, in "its attempt to efficiently interface with the connective environment, the conscious organism appears to increasingly inhibit what we call sensibility. By sensibility I mean the faculty that enable human beings to interpret signs that are not verbal or can be made so, the ability to understand what cannot be expressed in forms that have a finite syntax."[21] What is lost is the capacity to operate as a living human being who occupies the role of citizen-subject and engages in something like rational critical debate in relation to a set of environmental conditions understood to be real. The subject of global digital capital is a subject of an inhuman, abstract, and fundamentally unreal dimension that stands in for life. All of this leaves us with a "normality of a humanity that has lost all relation with what used to be human and that stumbles along looking for some impossible reassurance, searching for a substitute for emotions which it no longer knows."[22] This reassurance comes in the form of the Aspiration card which situates humans within the context of a digitally created global community, performs digital actions toward combatting climate change, and offers the comfort of digital consumption via the infinite path of global financial capital. This last path creates the final mode of capture for what remains of a living form of life.

The coup de grace of the Aspiration card is the process by which the interpassive pseudo-action captures individuals within financial capital. To plant the tree, we must use a credit card, and that means entering into the debt relation. The debt relation involves far more than individual debt. In fact, the entire set of conditions described thus far are situated within the debt relation. Since use of the Aspiration card is necessarily a digital transaction, everything I have described is distilled into the smallest possible set of digital signifiers. The initial transaction exists solely as a digital signifier, the pseudo-action of planting a tree is marked by a digital signifier, and the endless set of spectacular relations that correspond to ideas of citizenship and environmental activism are nothing more than digital images of these ideals. The digital signifier stands as the signifier of condensation for everything. Global capitalism depends upon the exchange of signs to the extent that signs "become the universal merchandise, the general equivalent in economic perception."[23] This works for capital, and it works for the consumer. Anyone who uses the Aspiration card will ultimately see nothing but signifiers of the actions they believe they have performed. Since global capital operates according to the logic of the debt relation, there can be nothing else but signs to stand in for what is only ever the monetization of an abstraction.

Perhaps the most far-reaching dimension of the kinds of things we see in the Aspiration card is the invitation and indeed condition to become immersed in the system of debt. The system of financial capital is the dominant mode of capitalist culture, and I will get to this, but at this stage what we see is the pathway by which individuals gain access and become captured by this system of exchange and cultural domination. By participating in the plant a tree program with the Aspiration card, we must take on the credit card with all that this entails. We enter into a credit relation with a massive corporate entity. There are, of course, an entire field of conditions that must be met in order to allow a person to enter into this contractual relationship. I will get to this below. What we need to make clear is that the credit relation and subsequent transactions which solidify this relation are part of the global capitalist system that creates a rigorously defined form of life and a specific type of subject within this system. This form of life, and the type of subject that emerges from this, propels Homo economicus and Homo consumptor into another mode of being. As Maurizio Lazzarato explains: "Credit or debt and their creditor-debtor relationship constitute specific relations of power that entail specific forms of production and control of subjectivity—a particular form of *homo economicus*, the 'indebted man.'"[24] The debt relation inherent in taking on the Aspiration card is not just a simple matter of spending money so as to do your part to fight global climate change and establish your status as a global citizen. Or, rather, you do establish your status as a global citizen, but this is not as simple as being a free participant. When an individual enters into this relation, they enter into a system of global capital which is far more than a simple relationship of buying things and paying later.

Financial capital determines the ways cultural relations unfold and the kinds of individuals who are able to exist within this system of economic and cultural production. As industrial capital faded in much of the Western world after the 1970s and 80s, finance banks emerged as the predominant owner-class within the rapidly changing system of global capital. What were once the investors and financiers of industry, the financial backers of the owner class, were transformed by the shifting terrain of neoliberal economic policies into a very different position with respect to culture. These financial backers have stepped forward to become the engine of global capital:

Finance, banks, and institutional investors are not mere speculators but the (representatives of) "owners" of capital, whereas those who were once "industrial capitalists," the entrepreneurs who risked their own capital, have been reduced to the "functionaries" ("wage-earners" or those paid in company stock) of financial valorization.[25]

Financial speculation and debt now control the economic and cultural systems that function within this economy. What Lazzarato identifies in his analysis is the fact that this transformation of capital, driven by neoliberal politics, has created a power relation that determines the way subjectivity is formed within our current cultural conditions: "What we reductively call 'finance' is indicative of the increasing force of the creditor-debtor relationship," and this relationship "has expanded its hold over all other social relations."[26] One of these social relations is the system by which individuals perform interpassive pseudo-actions and identify as global citizens by deferring to a finance corporation to perform their actions in combatting global climate change.

The obvious fact of what the Aspiration card promises is that individuals are first and finally consumers buying things with a credit card. That is all. The promises of combatting climate change and acting as a global citizen are mystifications and nothing more. Yet, the example of the Aspiration card is emblematic of a system of global capital that captures the desires of individuals within relations of pure spectacle and completely transforms them into Homo consumptor such that any contact with something we might call "real" is thoroughly removed from lived life. In fact, the Aspiration card is emblematic of global capital that fundamentally destroys human relationships and the environment within which our very lives are embedded. It is the systems of financial capital and semiocapital, no matter the lofty claims of credit card companies, that are eroding the conditions of life itself. As Bifo explains: "The financial cycle is bleeding the social environment dry: sucking energies, resources, and the future. And giving nothing back. Recovery of the financial process of valorization of capital is totally separated from the cycle of material production and social demand. Financial capitalism has achieved autonomy from social life."[27] The very system that promises access to global citizenship is precisely the engine of global decay. Individuals are atomized and divided monads within a system that produces indebted consumers—slaves to both the drives of consumer capital and the system of dept that makes it possible. We are so removed from even the money we spend that all civic engagement is now at a level of remove from material realities that anything like rational critical debate cannot even be conceived of, much less take place in something like a public sphere populated by living humans. All of this is experienced as a spectacular unity but consists of nothing but endless division.

Modern society consists of this elemental division in which unity can be perceived by virtue of the split in society itself. Laclau names the relation between division and unity as one of the key features of populism in which a society splits "into two camps—one presenting itself as the part which claims to be the whole," and those others who are perceived by the populist camp as others to be isolated and either corrected or eliminated.[28] The difference under the society of the spectacle is that this central division is itself a spectacular division. It does not consist of a different set of material conditions which determine the lived lives of individuals; it is the set of images which give rise to the perception of difference where in fact there are no differences at all. In fact, the spectacle effaces all real difference in favor of a consuming public who identify difference according to consumer choice rather than according to the material conditions of their lives. When Debord states the division is presented as unity, he describes division as a condition of the set of "free choices" offered by the spectacle by which one can recognize division among those who are given the same choices. We are nothing but consumers, and all difference is effaced by our status as consumers. As he explains further: "Struggles between forces, all of which have been established for the purposes of running the same socioeconomic system, are thus officially passed off as real antagonisms. In actuality these struggles partake of a real unity."[29] The unity is the unity of subjects of consumer capitalism whose only free choices are given ahead of time by a spectacular system of images which mediate individuals' relationship to their material conditions of existence. Rather than recognizing the essential sameness of everyday life in which all of life is reduced to the banality of consumerist fantasies, individuals see only the spectacular image of a set of false differences projected back to them in the form of a seemingly endless variety of differences.

The twenty-first century has accelerated and fractalized these conditions at an exponential rate to the point at which differences are manufactured endlessly and disseminated at the speed of light through the digital realms. The spectacle as it has been accelerated and fractalized by semiocapitalism now penetrates into the deepest realms of human thought, experience, and everyday life. We can see where Bifo is heading when he states that the Marxian concept of the "general intellect," or "the ability of knowledge to act as a value-producing force" has been incorporated into "the system of machines."[30] Where this leads us is a set of conditions in which the unity in division and division in unity that characterizes the society of the spectacle is now functioning within an "infinite brain-sprawl, an ever-changing mosaic of fractal cells of available energy."[31] It is within this matrix of fractalization that something like spectacular politics unfolds on the very same level as every other form of consumer choice which circulates within and around global financial and semiocapitalist modes of spectacular life. To enter into this in any way is to give over to the conditions of this fractalized and spectacular realm.

Under these conditions, to believe is to consume. Beliefs are substantiated to the degree that they can circulate within spectacular life and culture. The very ground of things like religious faith and political conviction is gone since the conditions by which individuals derive such things is thoroughly abstracted with the society of the spectacle exponentially accelerated by digital connection over human conjunction. Rational critical debate is replaced by interpassive performances enacted through a smartphone. The citizen-subject is an isolated and abstract monad within global financial and semiocapital, and the citizen-subject gains access and legitimacy through a screen that forecloses all human contact. The example of the Aspiration card works so well because it encapsulates a mode of engagement that is nothing but a consumerist movement within the debt relation whereby individuals can experience the pseudo-belief that they are acting toward ameliorating global climate change as a global citizen when in fact they are doing nothing but buying things with abstract digital signifiers of the absence of money. It should come as no surprise that a celebrity finance capitalist emerged as the paragon of contemporary politics in the United States. Who better than an artificially generated reality television star who exists entirely due to inherited wealth to lead the way in a world in which political commitments and affiliations are evaluated and determined by empty purchasing power. The celebrity who captures the public imagination exists in the same category as all other commodities. To have a political opinion operates at the same level as one's preference for a pickup truck or an EV, and one's political beliefs are as exchangeable as any other commodity. To be a "conservative" or a "liberal" is indistinguishable from everything else available on the Internet.

The commodification of belief and personal investment in belief cuts two ways. On the one hand, everyone and anyone can feel secure in the knowledge that they have performed their role as a citizen-subject simply by spending their money appropriately and by engaging in economically defined modes of interpassivity. The Aspiration card offers this spectacular form of subjectivity on a grand scale. On the other hand, the fact that one's status as a citizen-subject is defined by the degree to which you can engage and participate renders this a system of exclusion and alienation that is profound and final. A form of subjectivity that is completely defined by an abstract digital economic mode of empowerment necessarily excludes virtually everyone who cannot fully engage this system.

Notes

1.   HarvardPolitics.com.
2.   Webb, Jeanette. "Climate Change and Society." 115.
3.   Webb, Jeanette. "Climate Change and Society." 121–122.
4.   Debord. *The Society of the Spectacle*. 29.
5.   Pfaller, Robert. "Interpassivity and the Theory of Ritual."
6.   Zizek, Slavoj. https://www.lacan.com/zizek-pompidou.htm (Accessed 6/1/2021).
7.   Habermas, Jurgen. *The Structural Transformation of the Public Sphere*. 83.
8.   Foucault, Michel. *The Birth of Biopolitics*. 269.
9.   Debord. *The Society of the Spectacle*. 13.
10. *Biopolitics*. 256.
11. Hardt and Negri. *Empire*. 103. I should be clear that I am not relying on a naïve or essentialist mystification of the fact that what we call "the people" has historically been an expression of a narrow segment of society, that the people have been defined by an economically empowered white, male, heteronormative population. Rather, "the people" have functioned in line with Gramsci's theory of hegemony in which large portions of the social body are compelled to give "consent in the life and activities of the state and civil society" (*Gramsci Reader*, 194).
12. Hardt and Negri. *Empire*. 104.
13. Hardt and Negri. *Empire*. 188.
14. Hardt and Negri. *Empire*. 188.
15. Hardt and Negri. *Empire*. 188.
16. Hardt and Negri. *Empire*. 321–322.

17. Bifo. *After the Future*. 40.
18. Bifo. *After the Future*. 40.
19. Bifo. *After the Future*. 40 (emphasis added).
20. Bifo. *After the Future*. 41.
21. Bifo. *After the Future*. 41.
22. Bifo. *After the Future*. 41.
23. Bifo. *After the Future*. 100.
24. Lazzarato, Maurizio. *The Making of the Indebted Man*. 30.
25. Lazzarato, Maurizio. *The Making of the Indebted Man*. 21.
26. Lazzarato, Maurizio. *The Making of the Indebted Man*. 23.
27. Bifo. *After the Future*. 140.
28. Laclau, Ernesto. *On Populist Reason*. 83.
29. Debord. *The Society of the Spectacle*. 34.
30. Bifo. *After the Future*. 129.
31. Bifo. *After the Future*. 130.

Spectacle of Error

The past 20 years has seen a 20% drop in church membership. This follows a period from about 1937 to 1999 when church membership was sustained at over 70%. According to Pew Research, the percentage of those "who describe their religious identity as atheist, agnostic or 'nothing in particular,' now stands at 26%, up from 17% in 2009."[1] The UK *Daily Mail*, citing Pew Research, reported there are 1.5 million people in the United States who claim to be witches or Wiccans. At the same time, the United States has witnessed a messianic wave of Evangelical activism surrounding the rise of former President Donald Trump. It is an understatement to describe American Evangelicals as hypocritical. That the self-designated defenders of traditional morality and family values have rallied around a man who openly makes fun of people with disabilities, carries on with prostitutes and porn stars (and pays them off for their silence), and is arguably the most hateful person to ever occupy the office of the President of the United States is proof enough that American Evangelical Christianity is invested in things that have little to do with Christianity or even religion. But this is to miss the point. Evangelical Christianity, like every other capitalist venture, is capable of reconciling itself to anything or anyone since the conditions of possibility for anything that resembles faith are utterly erased. The demonstrably bankrupt pseudo-beliefs of American Evangelicals are precisely what are at the heart of the problem with things like belief and faith altogether. Evangelicals are not hypocrites because they fail to adhere to the dictates of their own religion. Rather, they are embodiments of the poverty of religion and faith in the twenty-first century. No one believes anything because the conditions for belief itself have been supplanted by the logic of consumer capital that dominates every aspect of contemporary life. What we now witness are the formal dimensions of belief without any of the substance of belief. The form of belief remains as it adheres to the logic of acquiring things as the singular marker of being in the world, while the contents of this form have become empty spaces to be filled with the same disposable contents as any other consumer commodity. Form of belief remains; belief itself is lost.

The distinction between belief as it has historically functioned and the form of belief is to be found in the origins of something like public opinion as it came to function in giving legitimacy to community, "the people," and the civic arena more generally. In its conventional form, belief, or opinion, was grounded in a civic body made up of private citizens who were oriented around a common set of public concerns. This originated in the seventeenth and eighteenth centuries as public opinion emerged into what is now known as the public sphere. Habermas traces the prehistory of opinion and explains that public opinion fully emerged at the end of the eighteenth century as opinion was transformed from a pejorative term to a feature of public legitimacy: "the opinion of the public that put its reason to use was no longer just opinion; it did not rise from mere inclination but private reflection upon public affairs and from their public discussion."[2] Absolutely central to this historical phenomenon are the use of reason and public discussion. In the contemporary suburban metropolis, the use of reason has been nullified by the complete acquiescence to images of thought rather than deliberation. The isolation of the sprawling suburban metropolis has completely foreclosed any possibility of public discussion other than in the form of isolated online posturing and recycled thoughts in the form of memes. The very conditions which gave rise to opinion and the belief systems on which opinions were formed no longer exist. As a result, what we see are virulent and even violent demonstrations of belief and opinion which are in fact performances driven by irrational fears and the form of belief which must be enacted like a dance so as to render it formally understood. The churches mark their legitimacy by erecting the biggest statue of Jesus. Political conviction is flagged with social media posts, bumper stickers, and public displays of weaponry.

It is in the realm of the truly mundane where the impossibility of belief is most pernicious. Where the "ordinary people" operate and live as if they are somehow outside of it all and more closely attuned to what decent folks believe. But it is here that the spectacle has so completely permeated life that even the most ordinary and mundane practices have become empty, meaningless, and bloodless—where the most ephemeral and ethereal features of life and spirit become empty gestures sutured to external and histrionic performances of that which has no substance. The lack of belief creates the need for spectacular demonstrations of belief. It is not idealism or a do or die commitment to a cause that fuels contemporary belief; it is the complete lack of belief that fuels dramatic outbursts. Rather than idealism and faith, these histrionic performances signal the nihilism and radical misanthropy which drive our contemporary world.

I have written elsewhere that the very geography of contemporary American life and culture is one that expresses the conditions of a null existence, that the culture of consumerism and the society of the spectacle has reached an apex in American cultural life in which the ground on which people live is an empty space that functions as a conduit for consumption and nothing else.[3] The geography of American life has become an environment of abstraction. The Real—any idea of the Real—which may have once existed has been plowed under and replaced by abstract forms of geography designed entirely to facilitate a culture of pure consumption, a culture which produces nothing but consumption and waste.

Consumer capital is all there is, and virtually all of life is subsumed by consumer capital. Basic needs are provided through a diffuse network of supply which is so far removed from the sources of food, fuel, electricity, and water that all of these things seem to simply appear ex nihilo. The massive waste generated by this world is also removed and landfilled in regions largely cut off from the lives and businesses which generate the waste. Once dumped, it no longer exists. The super-highway interstate system makes all of this possible. A vast system of interstates connects the entire country via a network of space which provides nothing but the means to move past it. The space of the interstate system is nothing but space to be overcome. The sole reason for its being is to pass it behind. The interstate system and the worlds which develop along its length and breadth are heterotopias, abstract spaces on which abstract lives are lived in relation to a world which grows ever more abstract. What is the highway but a space of abstraction in which "(t)he undifferentiated daily flow is punctuated only by the statistical, foreseen, and foreseeable series of *accidents*, about which THEY keep us all the better informed as we never see them with our own eyes—accidents which are never experienced as events, as *deaths*, but as a passing disruption whose every trace is erased within the hour."[4] As the highway effaces all difference through its endless uniformity and totalizing program of mathematical planning and control, everything else becomes undifferentiated to the point that what marks one "thing" apart from another is lost. Accidents and real deaths are experienced only as transitory moments in which the ceaseless flow becomes momentarily interrupted. And as all space becomes continuous in a seamless flow of undifferentiated space, space itself is lost. Designed to facilitate the movement over distances, "the pure space of the highway captures the abstraction of all *place* more than all distance."[5] This "all place" is also the multiple "places" in which everyday life is now lived in the abstraction of space. Suburban sprawl is pure abstraction laid out in accordance with the abstraction of the highway.

All of life is "presided over in unmediated fashion by the requirements of consumption."[6] What of the culture of this world? What emerges within this landscape of nullity is a new form of peasantry, one which is conditioned entirely by the logic of consumer society. Unlike the old peasantry in which natural ignorance was a function of an isolated world, the new peasantry is conditioned to their ignorance by a cultural logic which denies anything exterior to consumer culture. In this landscape of consumerism,

> Natural ignorance has given way to the organized spectacle of error. The "new towns" [subdivisions] of technological pseudo-peasantry are the clearest indications, inscribed on the land, of the break with historical time on which they are founded: their motto might well be: "On this spot nothing will ever happen—and *nothing ever has.*"[7]

An organized spectacle of error is the inevitable result of a population who derive all knowledge of the world from within the spectacle. As images and commodities provide the mediating force by which individuals experience their life-worlds, any knowledge of their life-worlds is completely conditioned by the unreality of consumer capital. Nothing can be known except insofar as it is represented in a consumable form that is exchangeable with any other commodity. Therefore, knowledge itself is a commodity, and if it is not commodified knowledge, it is not knowledge. The break with historical time comes about, at least in part, from the ex nihilo fashion in which these communities spring up around consumer culture and consumer culture springs up around these communities. The process is one of expressive causality. One aspect of consumer life does not precede the other. The entire landscape and culture of the American landscape now simply appears on the horizon complete with everything I described above and much more. Any history of the regions which may have preceded the creation of the consumer landscape is denuded with the very land on which the spaces are built. Since this historical narrative is completely negated, any narrative of the existence of these regions is created from within the same cultural logic by which they come into being. Nothing ever happened here because everything happens exactly the same way every minute of every day. Nothing will ever happen here because everything that could happen is a reproduction of everything else that has ever happened. The term peasantry seems appropriate since what we see in the people whose lives are defined by these regions and the forms of culture which define these regions consist of a population which lives in total ignorance of what is beyond the society of the spectacle.

By completely homogenizing space to the point that space itself has become meaningless, individual places have become abstractions. There is no longer any historical relation between the place and the geographical point on which that place is located. Since all places are interchangeable and exchangeable, no place has any value or relevance. The place of sovereignty which has historically defined communities has been displaced by a de-localizing logic of the interstate and homogenization of commerce in the forms of consumer capital. Every community is effectively identical. The town, the country village, and the city itself have become one suburban metropolis. With this, local power and sovereignty have also been displaced and dispersed across a non-localizable no-place. All life now resides in a literal "*ou-toupia*, or really a non-place."[8] Any and all historical narratives which gave rise to a sense of identity in the non-place of the contemporary suburban metropolis have likewise faded and been subsumed by the fleeting narratives of image-time and pseudo-cyclical time. As the Invisible Committee has shown, "The loss of experience and the loss of community are one and the same thing, seen from different angles."[9] In the absence of community and in the absence of anything that resembles real experience, the void is filled with nostalgic projections tinged with the irrational fears of the contemporary suburban metropolis—the fear of everything and anything which does not readily conform to the spheres of isolation and homogeneity that characterize contemporary life. Most importantly, the most potent threat is anything that may hold up a mirror to the empty void of contemporary suburban life. The ground of belief is replaced with the image of belief no matter how ridiculous or insane.

Further, what emerges in place of history, instead of a sense of place, and with the effacement of localizable seats of power are images of these lost threads of the social fabric. The substantive features of all these things are replaced by images of the thing which has been lost. Like naming streets after trees which were thoroughly removed, we end up with localities oriented toward places that do not exist. The narratives which undergird belief are gone, and in their place are flimsy and artificial substitutes. What is more, the traditional voices of power make no pretense that this is not the case. Since time itself has become the consumable image of time, the time of individuals and the time of meaningful historical narratives have been replaced by images of individual experience and history. The grand narratives that defined "America" perished long ago after Vietnam smashed the idea of the just war, as the greed and hedonism of the 1980s revealed America to be as much about cocaine as it was about family values, as non-white people all over the country called out the white middle-class as hypocrites for defending segregation while calling America the land of the free. In place of the grand narratives, we now have magnificent dramatizations of the grand narrative. America is the country which led the world to freedom in *Saving Private Ryan*. Even real war unfolds in the abstract non-space of the spectacle.

In the face of the nightmares of September 11, the President of the United States named the values that were under attack. Among his calls directly to the American people for support, Bush said, "I ask your continued participation and confidence in the American economy." Following the nightmare of the attacks on the World Trade Center, President Bush asked the American people to do their part by continuing to be engaged consumers. The role of the average American in support of the "War on Terror" was to continue buying things because consumption is what defines contemporary citizenship. Bush's characterization of the "terrorists" who directed the attacks—the motivation for their war on the world: "They hate our freedoms: our freedom of religion, our freedom of speech, our freedom to vote and assemble and disagree with each other." While the attackers are alleged to be engaged in a deadly battle with the fundamentals of democracy, the response of the ordinary citizen should be to maintain the flow of consumer commerce. The conflation of democracy and freedom with consumption of consumer goods could not be more direct. Yet, the language of the war effort and the images people are directed to idealize are the images of basic American freedoms. Be an active consumer, and you will fight the terrorists and maintain the American way of life. This was a triumphant moment for the society of the spectacle. It was here, at a moment of supreme crisis, that the leader of the free world announced and explicitly stated that freedom of religion, speech, and to vote and assemble has been completely subsumed by the absolute freedom to buy things.

Then the real wars George W. Bush unleashed on the world took place thousands of miles away from American soil. While real people were being blown to bits by drones and missiles, and IEDs, detonated with cell phones by what came to be known as enemy combatants, a term which took the place of enemy soldiers since it can be applied to virtually anyone who appeared to resist the United States, the average American watched the wars on CNN and Fox in between movies, reality TV shows, and situation comedies. The wars became part of the daily programming for everyday Americans. The entertainment industry cashed in quickly. Movies depicting the war in Iraq were hitting theaters by 2005. By 2008, *The Hurt Locker* won the Academy Award for Best Picture. The war itself instantly became consumable and patriotic Americans could do their part for the war effort by maintaining their civic duty as consumers by consuming things and by consuming images of the war. The horrors of war are completely removed from the everyday experience of the vast majority of people, and the enemy is neatly contained in an image of evil: the terrorist. The terrorist is a spectacular catch-all image of evil, it is the empty vessel in which the middle-class can understand what it is not. As Wark states: "The enemy that the spectacle can recognize is, once again, as in certain times past, the terrorist—the *spectacular* negation of the middle-class ideal."[10] This negation is only resolved to the extent that the positive existence of the middle class is retained in a purely negative projection that is nothing but spectacular imagery generated in the same entertainment industries that give us *American Idol* and *The Bachelor*. Things like war and its carnage are kept at a remove of not only geographical distance, but degrees of reality. There is no distinguishing between the number of the war dead, the latest standings in a reality TV show, QAnon, and Christian theology. Consumer capital provides the epistemological space for a mode of life that relies on acquisition over existence.

What we are left with is the stark absolutism of capitalism in the twenty-first century. The total Empire of the global capitalism and the spectacular screen of life on which we engage our fantasies of ourselves and our world. We are left with what Mark Fisher describes as capitalist realism, that state in which capitalism is all there is. The very conditions from which beliefs can be founded and expressed are collapsed into a cultural void of the consumer who sees the mirror of their being in the ritual spectacular consumption such that "(c)apitalism is what is left when beliefs have collapsed at the level of ritual or symbolic elaboration, and all that is left is the consumer-spectator, trudging through the ruins and the relics."[11] One need not, indeed, one dare not, attempt to believe what is beyond the spectacular image because it has thoroughly replaced all the flaws of the systems of belief which let us down in the past. One dare not venture over to a system of belief since "capitalist realism presents itself as a shield protecting us from the perils posed by belief itself."[12] And one does not need to venture over to the realm of belief since the spectacle and Empire provide belief for us.

Throughout the flattened and isolated space of the suburban metropolis where time unfolds in the abstract space of the image, real belief cannot exist because it does not need to exist. With the spectacle as the mode of existence and the ideological paradigm of contemporary life, everything about life comes in the form of what consumerist culture can deliver. What we consume becomes the definition of what we are, and this creates a way of living in which self-identity itself is a spectacular mirage. As the market has come to define life and more and more defines every aspect of life, "all community and critical awareness have ceased to be."[13] As we gather around in seas of sameness, community dies in the vacuum of interpersonal identification necessary for civic life. There is no need of community in any traditional sense of the term if community is given as a range of choices in shopping plazas, in automobiles in which we are isolated together, in school systems aligned with cartoon-like ideas of identity. Individuals as private citizens who engage in rational deliberation and discussion of public matters no longer exist. In fact, what we find are singular and isolated monads who consume ideas which have been fully formed to be consumable things. Public opinion and individual belief are received as commodities. As a result, substantive individuals are now either active consumers or non-entities. Your reality is determined by the extent of your engagement with consumer capital. Belief cannot function in the dialectic of the public and private spheres because what is now the public sphere is in fact privately owned and access is granted according to one's ability to participate in the single-directional process of consumption.

The civic arena is itself another commodified system which exists exclusively in name only. There are no civic spaces. The entire sense of community and all civic ideals are nostalgic projections made from a pastiche of long-gone rural idylls and small towns which were eradicated to make space for the suburban regions. The center of town which had historically been the geographical center in which private individuals engaged in public discussion has been replaced with the "Towne Centre" which is a shopping center anchored by a big box retail store and surrounded by other retail outlets. The suburban metropolis is the void of life where the image of life is broadcast back to isolated individuals who are no longer capable of committing themselves to an actual system of belief because the ideological ground on which belief is formed no longer exists. In its place is the spectacular image of cultural ideals, every imaginable form of spirituality, and the comforting homogeneity of other isolated individuals becomes both the other with whom one identifies, and the other to be treated with utmost suspicion. "The cumulative power of this autonomous realm of artifice necessarily entails a *falsification of life.*"[14]

The falsification of life is what has filled the vacuum with the loss of grand narratives which sutured individual belief to overarching forms of belief which acquired the status of universality. The signature feature of postmodernity in which "(t)he grand narrative has lost its credibility, regardless of what mode of unification it uses, regardless of whether it is a speculative narrative or a narrative of emancipation" has reached a different place with the total replacement for the grand narratives with facile images.[15] What is most telling about this is the evidence of these facile images right on the surface. The unreality which replaced the grand narrative is easily consumed and makes for an ideal pseudo-grand narrative. For example, something as common as the so-called "American Dream" in which the little person comes from nowhere to attain greatness has been replaced with idiotic displays of this dream in the form of *American Idol* and *America's Got Talent*. Hand-picked anybodies get to compete in a nationally televised talent show so the ordinary TV viewer can watch one of their own make the big-time. Not only has the grand narrative been lost, it has been replaced by a facile spectacle of a grand narrative which people then hold up as proof of a belief they know nothing about. In the vacuum of the loss of grand narratives, the suburban metropolis has been thoroughly seduced by images from popular culture as evidence of a lost cultural unity which can be regained. Just as Bush aligned the citizen at war with the committed consumer, and the great causes in Iraq and Afghanistan became "just like a movie," the institutions which guide culture have been subsumed by television versions of culture. The unreal reality of the suburban metropolis is dictated by the fanciful stories cobbed from TV and movies. Religion in America is dominated by fundamentalists clamoring for a more moral society which is aligned with the Bible. The voices of Christian fundamentalists have dominated public discourse for at least three decades now. And the cultural ideals these fundamentalists demand are nothing more than fanciful stories pieced together from television.

Notes

1. https://www.pewforum.org/2019/10/17/in-u-s-decline-of-christianity-continues-at-rapid-pace/ (Accessed April 8, 2021).

2.	Habermas, Jurgen. *The Structural Transformation of the Public Sphere*. 94.

3.	Templeton, Michael. "Null Space and Null Existence Under the Spectacle." https://www.hamptonthink.org/read/null-space-and-null-existence-under-the-spectacle

4.	Tiqqun. *This is Not a Program*. 152.

5.	Tiqqun. *This is Not a Program*. 152.

6.	Debord, Guy. *The Society of the Spectacle*. 123.

7.	Debord, Guy. *The Society of the Spectacle*. 124.

8.	Hardt and Negri. *Empire*. 190.

9.	Tiqqun. *Theory of the Bloom*. 54.

10.	Wark, McKenzie. *The Spectacle of Disintegration*. 112.

11.	Fisher, Mark. *Capitalist Realism*. 4.

12.	Fisher, Mark. *Capitalist Realism*. 5.

13.	Debord. *The Society of the Spectacle*. 21.

14.	Debord. *The Society of the Spectacle*. 45.

15.	Lyotard, Jean-Francois. *Postmodern Condition*. 37.

God, Inc.

Even as the Christian fundamentalists and Evangelicals claim to abhor the evils of contemporary society and profess to lead individuals toward a more moral and holy life, the world they want to "regain" never existed. It is not even a myth. It is pure television and Hollywood image. Christian fundamentalists in the form of the Evangelical movement are "re-creating what is imagined to be a past social formation based on sacred texts."[1] The absolute lack of a core set of beliefs drives the Christian fundamentalist movement to invent a core system of beliefs based on ideas which have no relation to actual historical facts. The stable, heteronormative nuclear family which is at the center of fundamentalists' assertions of moral superiority is in fact a creation of post-war television:

> (F)undamentalist visions of a return to the past are generally based on historical illusions. The purity and wholesomeness of the stable, nuclear heterosexual family heralded by Christian fundamentalists ... never existed in the United States. The "traditional family" that serves as their ideological foundation is merely a pastiche of values and practices that derives more from television programs than from any real historical experiences within the institution of the family. It is a fictional image projected on the past, like Main Street U.S.A. at Disneyland.[2]

For Hardt and Negri, this is evidence of an overall erosion of the systems of ideological investment which gave the conditions of possibility for the values and beliefs of Christian fundamentalists. That these groups have recourse to pure fictions, and not just any pure fictions but fictions on the order of Disney movies, is startling evidence of the lack of belief I am talking about. These are not beliefs; these are flimsy performances of belief based on still further juvenile performances of belief. A performance based on a fictional performance. Most significant is that the demonstrations or performances are in fact devoid of the declared faith on the part of the believers. The life devoid of life manifested in the contemporary suburban metropolis is also devoid of the possibility of real belief in anything at all. This void is continuously filled with readily consumable images of belief and faith. Like all other consumer commodities, it all becomes worthless the moment it is purchased and must be continually renewed.

And yet, the public declarations of these beliefs and even the willingness to fight over them have never been more prominent. This is a case in which the believers doth protest too much. The histrionic displays betray the absence of substance behind the demonstrations and declarations. One feels no need to claim that there is a war on their beliefs in the total absence of evidence of the existence of this war unless the war on your beliefs is of your own creation; a war you have invented yourself and aimed entirely at yourself. There is a built-in awareness to the vacuous absence at the core of fundamentalist Christianity. Not only do the believers betray a complete lack of faith, but their actual practices demonstrate their willingness to let others believe for them. Witness the multi-billion-dollar empire of Joel Osteen, who provides a nonstop thread of performances of faith and belief so that no one need bother with practicing faith themselves. Prayer lines and online devotions are available 24 hours a day, and seven days a week on top of Osteen's regular programming. One of the first things to notice about the Joel Osteen webpage is that it is a ".com" web location. It is a business, and at the top of the webpage is an advertisement for the latest books they have for sale. The top of the page offers a self-help book allegedly written by Victoria Osteen. The entire Christian enterprise of Joel Osteen is a completely commercial endeavor which places some version of Christian faith as the central focus of Joel Osteen. This is Christian faith fully mediated by consumer capital, and it represents the bedrock of faith for millions of people in the US and around the world.

Osteen is one of the most glaring examples of consumer faith. In the absence of any real belief, one can easily purchase belief from Osteen. Belief and faith come in discreet packages — books, videos, podcasts — you can even buy prayers from the website. Like hashtag participation, belief and faith are simple commodities which have taken the place of any real mental or emotional investment, and faith can now sit next to other commodities. The fact that one buys shares of faith in the name way one pays for Netflix or even Pornhub simply does not matter. Substance and reality are long gone from these transactions.

Perhaps the most comical example of the commodification of faith is the Ark Encounter. This is a theme park devoted to the biblical account of Noah and the Ark. It consists of a full-scale replica of the Ark purported to be built exactly to the specifications in the Bible.[3] There are life-sized figures of Noah and all the animals, a zip line, and a wooden food court (I suppose like the food court built by Noah). Everything about the Ark Encounter is a complete parody of religion but is consumed as if it were a real religious experience. So flimsy is the faith which underlies the Ark Encounter that you can be asked to leave for expressing any doubt about the veracity of their claims to truth. Ken Hamm, the man behind the Ark Encounter, makes a career out of capitalizing on the lack of faith which defines the contemporary suburban metropolis by providing an amusement park to supplement the lack at the core of all belief. Ark Encounter is a literal carnival of the spectacle. It represents the ultimate case in which real belief has completely disappeared and has been replaced by the image of belief. In this case, the images are so complete that people are able to interact with the images.

Osteen and the Ark Encounter are obvious cases which clearly demonstrate the loss of religious faith and the very possibility of belief. That large numbers of middle-class people (and all other demographics) can find points of identification with organizations that are so obviously capitalist ventures that have nothing to do with religion represents the extent to which the spectacle has colonized everyday life. Perhaps even more nefarious would be an example of something which poses as a completely benign and quasi-religious organization which is wide open and unallied with the fundamentalist politics that are intrinsically bound up with Christian fundamentalism. All over the country there are nondenominational organizations that grew out of the 1980s' and 1990s' turn from all organized forms of belief which had gone before. Crossroads Church perfectly captures the consumerist desire for a form of faith and belief that is completely oriented to the current form of life. It is a church for people who do not like church.

The most obvious external features of a Crossroads church are the distinctly modern, commercial architecture of the main building (it looks like it could easily be an Amazon distribution center), the massive parking lot, and the LED sign posted at the edge of the parking lot and the main road that advertises "Free Coffee." The coffee is good. I've had it. They know their clientele, these are people who are quite used to Starbucks, and Crossroads Church is able to provide them with the kind of product these people would demand. Even before you set foot in a Crossroads church or consult their highly sophisticated website, you see the external features of an undertaking which bears no resemblance to a traditional church. In fact, Crossroads Church is explicit on this last point. They are not a traditional church; they provide an alternative to the dogma of older models of Christian worship. The section of the website that states "Who We Are" explains:

We started the church for our friends who didn't like church.

Crossroads is for anyone who wants to seek God — from those exploring whether or not God even exists, to committed Christ-followers. We present biblical truths and show how they apply to our everyday lives. And we have a lot of fun while doing it.

A church for friends who do not like church, and you do not even need to believe in God. They welcome the fence-sitters, the so-called agnostics, maybe even the atheists. It is also a church with free coffee and an enormous parking lot for the masses of commuters. In the "Manifesto" they go on to say, "It's dark, it's loud, it smells like coffee. No, it isn't a hipster commune." To be fair, the manifesto explains that they, the members of Crossroads Church run after God. They claim to put God at the center of all they do and all they believe.

The actual substance of Crossroads Church consists of a massive media complex. It offers a YouTube channel, podcasts, music, livestreaming, etc. Crossroads Church is its own media empire built on their wide-open ideals of acceptance and God. Weekly services are built out on a grand theatrical performance complete with state-of-the art sound and lighting systems. Mixed media and live action performance enact and dramatize the message of the week's sermon. Video screens project clips from films and their own productions to accentuate the message. As part of your service to the church you can offer your computer skills to one of the many "Volunteer Roles" which support Crossroads Church. The organization is run by volunteers, but not just any volunteers. These are highly qualified technical volunteers — so technical that one entire group is devoted to "The Labs team" which "is on a mission to help navigate the course of how and what Crossroads does. We do that by collecting and transforming qualitative and quantitative data into actionable insights for our church leaders and staff." This is a marketing and PR firm built right into the church. Crossroads is a twenty-first century corporation that provides a theatrical supplement to belief for a new generation of consumers, highly sophisticated consumers who see themselves as being far too intelligent for the likes of Ken Hamm and Joel Osteen with their old-fashioned forms of old-time religion.

The weekly services are in fact theatrical performances of religious services. The Sunday services are multimedia productions which feature live drama and music, video projections, and fantastic light shows. (The media team is one of the volunteer opportunities.) The entire religious message is enacted on a grand scale for audiences who are used to *Star Wars* and huge live rock and roll events.[4] No boring sermons, no need to memorize stuffy catechisms, no drawn-out prayers (prayers are available on the website) — the process is performed for you. The fence-sitters and atheists are perfectly welcome because nothing will be asked of them. Nothing is asked of anyone other than to potentially volunteer your time and skills toward the church.

Crossroads Church is really just one among many. These mass-market churches for the contemporary middle class have sprung up all over the country, and most of them are in the sprawling suburbs amid mass consumerist destinations and parking lots that stretch out over acres of land. Mass pseudo-hip mega-churches have plowed over the old Pentecostal and Baptist churches that were once prominent in rural regions which have also been plowed under for the parking lots and consumerist destinations. McFaith for the sophisticated modern consumer. The electronic LED billboard at the edge of the parking lot of these churches (facing the interstate to attract the masses from the nowhere of daily life), there is always the advertisement for free coffee interspersed between the flashy graphics that advertise the weekly message. Many of these churches were borne out of the new pretense of sophistication projected by what we now call the urban hipster. The term and the phenomenon may be old news, but the figure that occupies this place in spectacular culture is not. They remain at the heart of contemporary youth culture, particularly that demographic that spends its money. These people are, in the words of the Invisible Committee, "the ultimate consumer of existence, the *hipster* lives within the confines of an endless experimentation *on himself*. Afflicted with a definitive lack of belief in humanity or in language, he has measured the volume of his being and decided never to go outside it, unless it's to ensure the self-promotion of his sterility."[5] This figure—I say figure because it is not a human in the zoological sense of the term, it is a caricature of life, a thing that is molded from the images of life that have taken the place of life—this figure is the ideal believer for the new suburban church of the spectacle. These figures are not capable of belief; what they require, before all else, is a space (cyber or otherwise) that offers precisely what Mark Fisher describes as a shield protecting us from the perils posed by belief itself.[6] Crossroads and its infinitely replicated derivatives are the ideal spectacular negation of faith and religion.

That Crossroads Church and the Evangelical grifters are capitalist ventures hiding behind the thin veneer of religious faith is a foregone conclusion. What is at issue is how the very idea of faith, and by extension, belief itself, has become so completely subsumed by the empty consumerist drives of the society of the spectacle—so completely subsumed that there is a real will to kill and die in the service of an artificial system of belief. On the one hand, the spectacular images of belief telegraph the lack of substance by their nature. At the same time, the complete lack of substantial belief appears to drive such a desperation behind individual expressions of faith that people are willing to believe there is some sort of war on faith, and they choose the word "war" quite deliberately. It is as if the loss of real faith and belief has precipitated a form of rage that must be expressed precisely because individual belief is now a thing of nothing. Like the no-place of the suburban metropolitan sprawl that proliferates along the highway system, and like the time out of time which characterizes the vapidity of everyday life, the insubstantial belief systems of contemporary society have begotten their own militant investments on the part of average middle-class people. As the foundation for real belief is evacuated of substance, the private investment in the image of belief must be publicly enacted in order to merit recognition as belief. This is to say that while individuals still claim to hold deep personal beliefs, they in fact do not even have access to these beliefs except insofar as belief is publicly displayed in the manner of a grotesque theatrical performance. This is the spectacular inversion of Greek theater as beliefs are projected back at a population in the form of images of beliefs. Where Greek theater performed the acts of the Gods so that individuals could participate in a communal belief, the contemporary absence of belief consists of an empty performance so that no one need ever participate in anything other than a passive consumption of preformed and predigested ideas. As with any other commodity, it becomes worthless the moment it is consumed and must be perpetually consumed again in order to renew itself. Communal participation is now isolated consumption. We gain access to the public sphere of communal belief via our isolated and private consumption of the image of public matters.

The historically delimited domains of the public and private spheres have undergone a radical displacement. This has everything to do with the dual conditions of the isolation intrinsic to the society of the spectacle and the unreality of the contemporary suburban metropolis. The public space has historically been the sphere of the political. This is the region in which individuals were exposed to each other and the world, and in which public discourse took place. In short, this is the realm of politics, in the most general sense of the term, and history. As public space has come under the exclusive private control in the form of huge corporate ownership, the public sphere has decreased. "The urban landscape is shifting from the modern focus on the common square and the public encounter to the closed space of malls, freeways, and gated communities."[7] We can see this quite obviously as the so-called "town center" has become nothing more than a name of an outdoor shopping mall. The "Towne Centre" is the name of a parking lot surrounded by retail and chain restaurants. It is emphatically not a public and civic space. These are the inevitable result of housing developments that are exclusively the domain of private corporate developers that dominate suburban sprawl, the spread of malls and strip malls as centers of public commerce, and the isolation of individuals in a land in which absolutely everything has become homogenized to the point of non-being. At the same time, individuals are increasingly isolated in their everyday lives as public space dwindles in accessibility. The public sphere has receded into invisibility as the private sphere has taken primacy as the dominant principle of everyday life and the suburban metropolis becomes nothing but "a series of protected interior and isolated spaces."[8]

With this, the grand historical narrative which once defined American life has fallen apart. The fundamental belief in ideas such as progress and the American Dream have broken apart under the epistemological erosion which long ago presented us with the postmodern condition. This is discussed above and much of this is old news. In the vacuum left behind by a complete collapse in the grand historical arc of American progress and in the vacuum of the loss of the public sphere, we find the spectacular performance of grand ideals and transcendent beliefs. The rise of fundamentalist Christians and the theater presented by Crossroads Church are all made possible precisely by the total lack of faith and belief which is the reality of contemporary life.

What is more, the sick core of fundamentalism is not the Christian Bible or any religious tradition. It is, in fact, the racist ideologies of isolation and separation which sustained the belief in white supremacy from the beginning of the nation. The imagined past perfection central to fundamentalist Christianity is not only patriarchal and heterosexual, it is also uniformly white. "Christian fundamentalisms in the United States have also continuously been oriented toward a project of white supremacy and racial purity. The new Jerusalem has almost always been imagined as a white and patriarchal Jerusalem."[9] The image of righteousness sold by Osteen and performed by the Ark Encounter, even the ostensibly benign religiosity of Crossroads Church, all of this is bound up in a spectacular performance of belief in the absence of real belief and in the elemental racisms which have characterized American life and culture from its earliest times. As the righteous pound the Bible on television and buy videos, podcasts, and books from professional Christians, what they are really buying are guarantees that their isolated lives which are utterly devoid of anything other than consumption and pollution will be preserved from the threats of racial impurity, sexual deviance, feminist castration, and foreign invasion. In short, the spectacular performance of belief is enacted to ward off that "*spectacular* negation of the middle-class ideal" identified by McKenzie Wark.[10]

In the total absence of place, in the negation of lived time that is the pseudo-cyclical time contained in eternal image time found on the Internet, the ground on which real belief can be formed is negated. Subjects are molded from within beliefs, not the other way around. In the world in which the fetishized free individual subject forms their own beliefs by effectively purchasing them online, what we end up with are expressions of fear and isolation commodified and neatly contained in safe images which mollify fear and isolation. In the suburban metropolis there is not ideology because the world self-evidently exists — this is the world in which "Everything that appears is good; whatever is good appears."[11] Therefore, that which remains foreign, different, distant, hidden, etc. is necessarily evil and threatening. What is more, no single individual need concern themselves with this in any meaningful way because the threats and foreign powers are handled by the spectacular performances of faith and belief which stand in for individual thought. That which is foreign, different, and distant remains hidden because it has not properly purchased visibility and therefore the right to exist in pseudo-public life. All belief and action takes place on an other scene — and I choose that term quite deliberately — as the internal realm of belief is externalized through the spectacle: "The spectacle's externality with respect to the acting subject is demonstrated by the fact that individual's own gestures are no longer his own, but rather those of someone else who represents them to him."[12] This is the central point at which the individual, and by extension the whole of contemporary life, is forever dislodged from the ground of real belief. The unconscious is now an external fantasy and individual dreams are consumed en masse through Netflix. Experience itself takes place exterior to the self. Community, then, disappears in the fog of a populace which cannot exist without individuals who actually live in the world. That which would appear to be an innate expression of humanity has disappeared as individuals hand over their humanity to spectacular performances of being, of faith, of belief. "Only a radical alienation of the Common could cause the innate Common to warp in such a way that solitude, finitude, and display, that is to say the only true tie between men, seems like the only possible tie between men."[13]

The reassertion of white supremacy comes as the isolation of contemporary life becomes most precarious, as the nonexistence of contemporary life is so completely universalized that the emptiness itself gives rise to age-old fears and hatreds. The cowardice of contemporary life can be assuaged through the mass participation in hatred and war fantasies which never threaten the everyday life of individuals whose lives are meaningless, where the void which threatens to consume the collective fantasies as they are played out on television, movies, the Internet, vapid advertising etc. threatens to overwhelm individuals who are powerless in the face of this void. The angry white men asserting their supremacy are in fact nullified non-beings who detest their nonexistence "where the spectacle's function in society is the concrete manufacture of alienation."[14] What has historically been the profound form of belief in religious faith is now nothing more than passive consumption of images of faith. The television evangelists have long been viewed as hucksters and con men, and there has never been a shortage of clownish sideshows like the Ark Encounter. What has taken over in the contemporary suburban metropolis is the mass participation in these types of cons to the extent that they now exert dominance over more mainstream forms of faith. The urban hipster can now find a place of worship in the slick multimedia productions at Crossroads Church, and the forms of faith which once exerted power in the form of the Ideological State Apparatus that is the church have been subsumed by corporate image machines which provide prepackaged faith and religious devotion. The same loss of real experience that attends the no-place of contemporary life finds its transcendent correlative in the image machine of God. Even death is now nothing more than an abstraction, and grief can be projected outward so as to forestall the experience of death and grief. All of belief is now performed in an endless carnival of a temporal heterotopia, one which is staged in such a way as to be a-temporal, eternal in the form of pseudo-cyclical time and placed in a no-place of a heterotopia; a paradox since the utopia of the contemporary suburban metropolis is in fact a no-place, in the literal sense of "utopia," but which functions like heterotopia in the form of a temporary carnival. Belief unfolds in the forms of "(t)hese heterotopias" which have all the markings of those "marvelous empty sites on the outskirts of cities that teem once or twice a year with stands, displays, heteroclite objects, wrestlers, snakewomen, fortune-tellers, and so forth."[15] Now, they teem with Evangelicals, white supremacists, and middle-class Americans who are unable to see the nonexistence in which they live because there is nothing external to this nonexistence.

Notes

1. Hardt and Negri. *Empire*. 147.
2. Hardt and Negri. *Empire*. 148.
3. The news outlet *The Conversation*, funded largely by public universities and claims to offer "trustworthy and informative articles," reported that the Ark Encounter is able to "go far beyond the Bible to explain Noah's training in shipbuilding, carpentry and blacksmithing." Yet, in 2019, Ark Encounter sued over flood damage to the Ark. The Tyvek insulation designed to protect the attraction failed. The owners are seeking compensation because the construction was not properly fitted to resist flood damage. That those who invest their faith and credulity in the Ark Encounter claim to find "truth in Genesis," while claims of historical veracity are at odds with obvious facts. Jain, Kalpana. "At a Popular Evangelical Tourist Site, the Ark Encounter, the Image of a 'Wrathful God' Appeals of Millions." *The Conversation*.
4. In 2008, a 23-year-old woman died in a fall during a Christmas performance at Crossroads Church due to an equipment failure. This event lives on through local news websites. The event is forever present in the pseudo-cyclical time of the image. One is able to eternally participate in the

tragedy in image-time. Prayers are also available through commercial websites. The eternal presence of the event also makes it possible for church consumers to live with the idea that the young woman made the ultimate Christ-like sacrifice. She is a martyr to the spectacular image of faith.

5.   Tiqqun. *Theory of the Bloom*. 51.

6.   Fisher, Mark. *Capitalist Realism*. 5.

7.   Hardt and Negri. *Empire*. 188.

8.   Hardt and Negri. *Empire*. 188.

9.   Hardt and Negri. *Empire*. 148.

10.   Wark, McKenzie. *The Spectacle of Disintegration*. 112.

11.   Debord. *The Society of the Spectacle*. 15.

12.   Debord. *The Society of the Spectacle*. 23.

13.   Tiqqun. *Theory of the Bloom*. 104.

14.   Debord. *The Society of the Spectacle*. 23.

15.   Foucault. "Of Other Spaces." 7.

Ruins and Relics of Ideology

Don Delillo's *Libra* is a triumph of conspiracy theories amid what could be seen as the central site of conspiracy theories: the Kennedy assassination. There are over 40,000 books on the Kennedy assassination, and many of them offer complex theories that support equally complex conspiracies about the assassination. Few things in American history have offered the conspiracy theorist more fodder for every imaginable set of possibilities. Delillo offers his own theory. The fact that it is fiction did not seem to be enough for George Will who declared the book a "work of literary vandalism and bad citizenship."[1] Perhaps what bothered Will more than anything else is that Delillo's novel is, in many ways, more believable than most of the other conspiracy theories in circulation. The novel itself takes account of conspiracy theories and offers good reasons for the allure. As the character Nicholas Branch, the man who assembles the facts from within top secret government channels, goes over the vast sea of materials that have accreted after the assassination, he thinks to himself: "There is enough mystery in the facts as we know them, enough conspiracy, coincidence, loose ends, dead ends, multiple interpretations. There is no need, he thinks, to invent the grand and masterful scheme, the plot that reaches flawlessly in a dozen directions."[2] The problem for George Will, and in the novel itself, is precisely that it is believable, that it provides enough coordinates for knowledge to latch upon to allow us to structure a sense of verisimilitude. There are enough reasons, there are enough absences of reasons even, to believe the conspiracies, and the facts themselves offer enough to believe the conspiracies. This is the central issue: belief can be supported, and it does not matter if the belief is wrong. What matters is that there is belief. Delillo's novel presents a problem for someone like George Will not because it presents us with a dangerous and false narrative of real events, but because it creates the very conditions that make it possible to believe something—anything. Such a narrative achievement is scarcely possible anymore.

Belief in the conspiracy theory requires a frame of understanding in relation to the material external world that supports belief. If this frame of understanding no longer coheres, belief itself cannot be supported. However, the psychological mechanism of belief remains even in the absence of belief itself. The kinds of conspiracy theories that now appear to dominate the popular imagination are of a different order. To be more precise, the exact nature of what attends the claims of belief that come with these conspiracies has been complicated by the ways knowledge and information are accessed, consumed, and circulated so that what now appears as belief lacks the epistemological and emotional investment required of belief. The reasons for this have to do with the spectacular ways people understand their life-worlds and the fundamentally inhuman ways we are compelled to interact with the infinite variety of information that forms the ideological construction of everyday life. As we have seen in the case of religious belief, the forms of belief that define contemporary political views are every bit as distorted and deformed.

The decrease in active membership in traditional Christian churches, the increase in the number of people who claim to be Wiccan or some other version of neopagan belief, coincides with the ascendancy of cultural phenomena exemplified by the QAnon conspiracy. There have always been fringe groups and fringe beliefs that claimed to know what the rest of us refuse to see before our eyes. One can argue that this is simply a feature of culture; that while the masses adhere to what is culturally safe, and the intellectual elite claim to have moved beyond these safety zones, there have always been that segment of society who has managed to reveal the REAL truth. By way of a working definition, Douglas et al. surveyed a variety of psychological investigations into the nature of conspiracy theories and the tendency of some to believe them as operating in a closed system of self-affirming belief: "conspiracy beliefs comprise part of a monological belief system where these beliefs comprise a self-sealing and expanding network of ideas that mutually support each other."[3] In short, conspiracies purport to provide explanations that are in advance of the official word, which is by definition suspect, and find proof in the fact that there is nothing outside the conspiracy theory. The conspiracy theory contains its own proof. There is a common joke that says that the reason we do not see elephants hiding in trees is because they are good at it. But again, these things have always existed. Historically it has been easy to dismiss these forms of belief and the people who adhere to them. In fact, the nature of the monological belief system is such that dismissing it is proof to the adherents that they are right and everyone else is blind to the truth. What is different with the rise of Q, and the comedy of disasters that have come with it, is the number of people, the percentage of the population who believe it and the kinds of people who believe it. We are no longer talking about the disaffected and the alienated as if these conditions can define a small and insignificant minority. Disaffection and alienation are now the fundamental conditions of life within the exponentially amplified society of the spectacle. In our current condition, the separation and alienation of the society of the spectacle have taken on dimensions which expand the forms of separation and alienation on a scale that is both accelerated and enlarged, and microscopic and internal.

The fundamental conditions that produced the society of the spectacle have been accelerated with the Internet and social media. Far more than anything Debord and the Situationists could have anticipated, we have moved into a state of being in the world in which the mediation of the image now moves at the speed of light. Not only do we interact with the image, but we are compelled to interact with the image as if it were a living feature of our lives. Reality itself is now a live real-time performance that operates according to a dynamic that creates the conditions of human interaction but in fact operates according to a completely different logic—a logic that is not human at all.

While the mediation of the image remains the cultural logic of consumer culture, a cultural logic which has captured everyday life absolutely, the transmission of the image has taken on dimensions that have further captured life. There is an antagonism at work in contemporary culture that involves the fundamental ways that human minds grasp their life-worlds and the machines of information that demand to be grasped according to a system of thought that is not human. Here we must return to the distinction made by Bifo regarding the human mode of understanding and the mode of information transmission and access that operates in the digital realm. This difference and antagonism (I use the term antagonism rather than antithesis because the differences at work here are irresolvable by definition and cannot be synthesized in the form of a different mode) consist of conjunction versus connection. Conjunction is an interaction that unfolds according to the moment-by-moment cues generated from within the interaction itself. Human beings will always bring modes of being, forms of language, prejudgments, personal biases, etc. to any instance of interaction, and none of these preexisting formations are capable to delimiting, predicting, or in any way totalizing the nature of the interaction. Connection is coded. It demands a pre-established mode of engagement and interaction, and anything that does not or cannot conform to the code is by definition incorrect. Conjunction is human. Connection is the digital realm of social media and Internet. Connection is coming to, or has already come to, dominate everyday life. Conjunction cannot engage this mode of interaction in the manner of conjunction and therefore inevitably becomes irrelevant.

Of critical importance here is that the fundamentally human mode of communication is becoming overrun and over-written by a mode of communication that is inhuman. The human mind simply does not function according to the mode of connection. We are capable of understanding this mode of communication, but the way we create and sustain social life as social beings is not connective and as we are over-written by connectivity, our ways of producing and creating our life-worlds are dangerously altered. This is not a case of the rise of the machines like *The Terminator* in which we produce machines that can destroy us. This is a case in which we have produced machine modes of understanding that are forcing us to communicate like machines in place of communicating like humans. The danger is not that the algorithms will take on a life of their own. The danger is that we are being forced to think like algorithms, and the algorithms are teaching us to think like them. When you see ads in your social media feed, has the algorithm learned to show you what you like, or have you learned to like what the algorithm shows you? The point here is not to move into apocalyptic scenarios, although these are well worth our attention. The point is to begin to recognize that when Debord defined social life as that which is mediated by the consumerist image, we have now moved on to a state in which social life is that which adheres to the digitally defined logic of digitally produced images. We now exist within a world of ideas by which we orient ourselves to our external world and each other via media imagery. The ways in which we cognitively access this imagery is running at a pace that is beyond us. This is an epistemological set of conditions, one in which both the forms of thought and the mode by which thought is delivered and accessed fundamentally exceeds human cognitive capabilities. As Bifo explains:

(D)igital technology is based on the insertion of neurolinguistic memes and automatic devices into the sphere of cognition, into the social psyche, and into forms of life. Both metaphorically and non-metaphorically, we can say that the social brain is undergoing a process of wiring, mediated by immaterial linguistic protocols as well as by electronic devices.[4]

These immaterial linguistic protocols do not, I would argue, supersede the society of the spectacle. Rather, they lift the society of the spectacle up toward a new plane of operation, and at the same time down toward a greater reach into the human sense of self. The mediating power of the image is exponentially accelerated while the ways in which individuals come to understand themselves in relation to their social worlds are pushed to exponentially deeper levels of alienation and separation. Not only are individuals alienated and separated from the material realities of their worlds, the worlds they live in have become increasingly unreal. These processes have created small microcosmic ecosystems of everyday life that sustain themselves on a plane of digital unreality that feeds on itself. Consumers are able to "freely" choose an ecosystem of thought and being that has no correlative outside the informatic bubble of digital images and meme information.

To be clear, what Bifo describes is not a simple matter of cultural influence. The movement toward connectivity over conjunction does not come down to a simple matter of a population that is somehow influenced by too much information. These conditions are far more complex. What Bifo describes is an epistemological and cognitive condition in which the ways we think are overwhelmed to the point that thinking itself is reoriented toward the demands of digital connectivity that is beyond human cognitive capacity under a regime of knowledge that is characterized as "cognitive wiring" in the capture and submission of life and mental activity into a "sphere of calculation."[5] I would argue that the key terms here are capture and submission. Mental and social life, including the everyday life of individuals, are captured within a regime of understanding which compels individuals to submit to this regime of understanding that is defined by the terms of the digital mode of connection which, by definition, cannot properly communicate via the human cognitive mode of conjunction. What we end up with are methods of capture that occur on "two different levels: on the epistemic level it implies the formatting of mental activity, on the biological one it implies the technical transformation of the processes by which life is generated."[6] The processes by which life is generated—social life or everyday life—translates to the ideological underpinnings of culture. Today, these underpinnings are unmoored from any common ground by which social life can be linked to the material workings of lived life. Rather, social life takes place in bubbles, or, as I stated above, within digital ecosystems of thought which are entirely abstract clouds of images and information which operate according to the logic of consumer capital—a hyper society of the spectacle. Just like an environmental ecosystem, these ecosystems of connective digitized social life produce their own environment, their own atmosphere, their own systems of generation and regeneration and subsequently cut themselves off from any other ecosystem that does not directly feed its cycle of life and regeneration.

In employing the term ecosystem I am not directly referencing Felix Guattari's theory of the "Three Ecologies." However, Guattari develops his idea of social ecology in a manner that lends itself to my thesis insofar as the social ecology comprises developments in the production of social and cultural life that are radically disrupted by contemporary global capital and spectacular culture. Guattari explains that the reach of global capital has penetrated every region of social life and de-linked subjectivity from all stabilizing practices:

Social ecology will have to work towards rebuilding human relations at every level of the socius. It should never lose sight of the fact that capitalist power has become delocalized and deterritorialized, both in extension, by extending its influence over the whole social, economic and cultural life of the planet, and in "intension", by infiltrating the most unconscious subjective strata.[7]

Crucial here is the deterritorializing power of social ecology to the extent that the territorial domains of thought and belief are no longer located within inter-human relations but are increasingly mediated and dictated by digital and connective relations that negate fundamental human modes of cognition. Among the points of cognitive and social access which are deterritorialized are the modes of communication by which communities are formed and the media by which information is transmitted. Information and understanding are no longer at least partially dependent on inter-human communication, but rather are entirely predetermined by electronic communication that is completely determined by connection over conjunction. As a result, communities are oriented toward the electronic modes of communication, its communicative logic, and the predetermined range of messages and ideas which can be counted as legitimate. Human interaction is removed from the process altogether.

These cultural and social conditions have their negative antithesis, and in order to grasp the dialectic of unreality as it is unfolding, it is necessary to bring about an old but sturdy concept. The processes of the production of social life and the forms of knowledge and belief that comprise social life can be understood under the broader concept of ideology. The fundamental ways in which individuals orient themselves to their worlds and to each other falls within ideology as an overarching concept. Althusser's definition of ideology still stands as a basic premise and I need to foreground and emphasize this: "THESIS I: Ideology represents the imaginary relationship of individuals to their real conditions of existence."[8] Althusser is deceptively simple in this short definition. His use of the term imaginary is quite specific. Without getting into a Lacanian digression, imaginary for Althusser is what individuals glean from the infinite flow of data that unfold in their lives. Of this infinite flow of data, humans can only access a limited amount and the ways this data takes on meaning is conditioned by the social practices of a given cultural moment. We access the "real conditions of existence" from within a socially, culturally, and historically conditioned set of beliefs, practices, values, etc., and whatever comprises the real cannot be known except through the filters of these imaginary relationships. Althusser's understanding of ideology is dependent, at least in some measure, on access to a life-world that exists in the material world. When we bring this definition of ideology to bear on a life-world that only exists as a connective digital epistemological ecosystem, we are now looking at the imaginary relationships to the artificially and digitally formatted conditions of existence. Since these ecosystems of thought and pseudo-being foreclose the possibility of anything external to consumer capitalist representations of the real conditions of existence, all other forms of thought and belief are equally foreclosed and inaccessible. Or, put another way, thought and belief are rendered irrelevant. This is what Mark Fisher means by capitalist realism in which "beliefs have collapsed at the level of ritual or symbolic elaboration, and all that is left is the consumer-spectator, trudging through the ruins and the relics."[9] The ritual and symbolic elaboration depends on a common understanding of what is being ritualized and symbolized. When ritual and symbol are drawn from purely fantastic—spectacular—images generated within an isolated and closed system of digital abstraction, there is nothing on which belief itself can be grounded. Therefore, belief is replaced with the performance of belief which can be played out in a cybernetic ecosystem that endlessly affirms and feeds itself.

Trudging through the ruins and relics becomes an exercise in the most individualistic expressions of personal freedom, one in which what one believes can be freely chosen from virtually any set of ideas that are in circulation no matter how fantastic or ridiculous. We choose what we believe in the same way that we choose Coke over Pepsi. In fact, the sources of belief are vulgar commodities indistinguishable from Coke or Pepsi. And under these conditions, what we believe takes on the same value as any other commodity, which is to say that belief has no value at all except insofar as beliefs are validated and circulated through spectacular digital media. Belief is legitimate to the extent that it can be rendered exchangeable within the digital ecosystem. What is valued is the mere fact of *having* a belief rather than the content or quality of a belief. Having a belief that circulates in the same manner as all other commodities within consumer capital renders belief meaningless except insofar as one is free to have any belief one chooses. At this level, what we believe becomes a matter of consumer choice, and what upholds belief depends entirely on the circulation of images and informatic bits as they are generated and disseminated via electronic media.

When we are living under a regime of culture that is largely or totally dominated by the definition of ideology given by Althusser, the conditions for belief in the broadest sense of the idea are still possible. Even false belief still coheres as belief. I am not interested in the substance of what people believe. It is a given that groups of people have subscribed to forms of belief that can be absolutely absurd. The point is that they believed. What is more, the psychology of things like conspiracy theories, millennial end of the world cults, or any other outlandish belief are not the issue. When the system of knowledge is fundamentally guided by an imaginary relation to the real conditions of existence, we can formulate beliefs. When the system of knowledge loses its ground and is dislodged from an imaginary relation to the real conditions of existence, the basis of belief itself is gone. It is not as if ideology as such disappears. What we have is an ideological paradigm that is formed out of imaginary relations that are constructed from prefabricated imaginary relations. This is not necessarily a condition in which people are deluded or brainwashed into believing things that are not true. Rather, the case I am making is that the frame of understanding from which belief itself is formulated is becoming undone.

To get a better sense of where this is leading, we should return to the basic definition of the spectacle. Debord explains in Thesis 4: "The Spectacle is not a collection of images; rather, it is a social relationship between people that is mediated by images."[10] A social relationship mediated by images produces an ideology of imaginary relations to the fundamental unreal conditions of existence. Althusser's definition of ideology must be extended to include the conditions of existence under the regime of the society of the spectacle. Althusser's understanding of the "real conditions of existence" depended upon a model of the common that was oriented to experiences as they unfold in the world. Put another way, real conditions of existence were at least largely made up of what people lived through in their everyday lives which included interactions with other individuals, the conditions of life in streets, farms, suburbs, etc., and every other real condition as they are understood in their imaginary relation. With the rise of the spectacle, these real conditions of existence are ever more mediated by systems of the image that render "real conditions" increasingly abstract and always already situated in an imaginary relation that precedes individuals. Thus, Debord explains that the spectacle functions as "both the outcome and the goal of the dominant mode of production," and the dominant mode of production is consumer capitalism.[11] Further, the way that spectacular culture functions renders it at "the very heart of society's real unreality."[12] This clearly resonates with Althusser's definition of ideology insofar as this real unreality now takes the place of the real conditions of existence. We could restate the definition as: Ideology represents the imaginary relationship of individuals to their status as consumers of the images which stand in for a semblance of the real conditions of existence. All that could possibly stand in for "real conditions" are now a function of pre-coded data that situates imagination in a fundamentally unreal and unassimilable system of semiotic exchange.

However, all of this needs to be further adjusted. We are not just dominated by the society of the spectacle. Culture and society have been further abstracted by the rise and dominance of semiocapitalism and cyberculture. In Thesis 13 Debord raises a crucial feature of the spectacle which has now become a central feature of life and belief. Social arrangements are now situated in a state of absolute passivity, but Debord first raises the flag of what will become a signal feature of everyday life when he explains that "(t)he spectacle is essentially tautological, for the simple reason that its means and its ends are identical. It is the sun that never sets on the empire of *modern passivity*."[13] The spectacle situates individuals in a passive relation to the forms of knowledge and information they received and subsequently employ to represent the conditions of everyday life. Since the forms of knowledge and information are completely defined by the logic of consumer capital, these forms of knowledge and information are images of the real conditions of existence as they are distorted to further the expansion of consumer capital. However, the contemporary world has exploded the passive relation of individuals toward something far more extreme.

In order for passivity to coexist with an individualistic sense of freedom and self-will, the ideological construction of spectacular culture must impart a mystification that the choices individuals make are free choices and carry the same weight as any other choice toward a faith in self-authorization. In other words, people need to have a basic faith in the idea that they are rational actors in the world even as their range of choices are increasingly limited by a system that thoroughly obfuscates the "real conditions of existence" and offers a range of choices that are prescribed ahead of their choices by a global system of commodity capital whose sole purpose is to produce and reproduce consumers. Thus, the regime of consumer capital and the society of the spectacle "entails a generalized shift from *having* to appearing: all effective 'having' must now derive its immediate prestige and its ultimate raison d'etre from appearance."[14] What appears is what is, and one's place in the world and range of "free" choices consist of what appears as being and appears as a choice. The materiality of lived life is negated in favor of an appearance of life. Individuals sense their freedom by the range of images they are free to choose from. Still further, reality itself disappears behind a mystification that denies the real conditions of existence by replacing them with images of existence which mediate between individuals and their worlds:

> At the same time all individual reality, being directly dependent on social power and completely shaped by that power, has assumed a social character. Indeed, it is only inasmuch as individual reality *is not* that it is allowed to appear.[15]

Individual *reality* is not! What stands for social reality is the infinite array of images, images that are stitched into the system of consumer capital, which provide the image and appearance of reality such that any and all experience of reality is of the order of fantasy. The very concept and act of choice is situated in a fundamentally unreal position, and the basis of any choice is itself an unreal reality.

For us to believe something—anything, we need to find a basis and a frame of thought for that belief. This is easy to see when we look at a system of knowledge and belief that is either unfamiliar or historically distant. Foucault demonstrates how the old system of correspondences and resemblances functioned just fine for centuries. This paradigm of meaning and belief unfolded in a manner that was self-evident in that "resemblance is visible ... in the network of signs that crosses over the world from one end to the other."[16] With the emergence of empirical thought, scientific method, exchange, and classification, these older epistemic orders eroded and a different order of knowledge ascended. If we examine the order of knowledge and belief within the society of the spectacle, we do not see the emergence of different order of knowledge and belief. What we see are the conditions for knowledge and belief fade into a system of appearance such that belief loses its foundation. If what is "true" becomes a matter of choice among a vast range of other choices, and what is real is only what appears as real, then one can easily dispense with orders of truth and reality that are not valuable within a system of consumer choice. We are no longer interested in ideas and bits of information that are true. We are only interested in ideas and bits of information that have value as things which can be exchanged as so many other commodities. Questions of truth and reality are devalued in favor of ideas and forms of knowledge which perform in the markets of truth and reality. One never questions whether an idea is true. The question is only, "How can I use this idea?" Again, I am not interested in what various people and groups believe. I am concerned with the basis of how it is possible to believe, and under the conditions described thus far, the basis of belief itself is eroded. Even as individuals and groups advance beliefs of all kinds—the nation, God, specific religions, etc.— the foundations for these beliefs are falling away. I will get to this below, but there is a consistent rise in histrionic displays of belief as the foundation of belief itself disappears. The more noise we make about our beliefs, the less we believe anything at all, and the more the histrionic display gives legitimacy to non-belief because histrionic displays can be captured, reproduced, and infinitely circulated in the digital ecosystem. The sound and fury of contemporary political movements are the markers of a population that doth protest too much because the theatrical performance of protest is of more significance than the substance of belief. What matters is that you gain attention in the form of hits on YouTube, likes on Facebook and Instagram, and shares on Twitter. Your political movement, your social struggle, your religious faith—all are measured by the metrics of social media and ratings. You obtain legitimacy through Search Engine Optimization and social media traffic.

"... what is still there..."

What I have described so far is not a progression. These conditions compound upon themselves to produce a cultural and social state in which the foundations that make it possible to genuinely believe anything are eroded to a point that something else takes the place of belief itself. What we are left with is the fundamental impossibility of belief even as the performance of belief has grown more widespread. But in the course of everyday life, belief has been taken over by digital mechanisms which believe for us. As Bifo explains:

In our contemporary situation, marked by the infinite expansion of the infosphere—and in particular of economic and financial information—rational elaboration and political decision-making are no longer within reach of individual or social organizations. As a result, democracy has been replaced by automatic procedures, by algorithms and devices for automatic selection and recombination whose general rationale is the replication of the capitalist form.[17]

Individuals no longer need to express beliefs in any meaningful way since the digital realm allows them to discharge the social investment through the empty sharing of memes, hashtags, and anything else available on the Internet. I can easily prove my faith in God and country by sharing a meme which clearly expresses my firm belief in God and country. Clearly, I am committed to transgender rights because I follow a number of pages on social media which claim to support transgender rights. On and on ... What is more, the algorithms and devices for digital selection insulate individuals from any and all responsibility and/or consequences from what they express and the "beliefs" they claim to be behind these expressions. The so-called insurrection on January 6, 2021, is an excellent example. Moskalenko and McCauley point out that QAnon is a largely debunked conspiracy theory and poses no real threat to democracy. However, they do state that QAnon and the events of January 6th demonstrate "the radical means that some Americans are willing to use to advance their political views."[18] I contend that these events reveal the contrary. They reveal the level of unreal and delusional fantasies that stand in for what we once called belief. What is important is large numbers of people claimed to believe in QAnon (or still do adhere to this conspiracy), and many of these people were motivated to storm the United States Capitol Building on January 6th in an effort to stop the certification of the election of President Biden. But any evidence of a substantive belief disappears in the face of what these people actually did. The so-called storming of the Capitol, though replete with very real consequences up to and including death, was a collective performance that brought utter shock even to those who participated.

A stellar example of what I have been spelling out here comes after the events of January 6. Over the course of weeks and months, authorities arrested numerous people. The reactions of those arrested and charged for their actions during the insurrection has been shock. These people cannot believe there have been very real consequences for their actions. It is not that these people believe they did nothing wrong. It is that they do not believe they did anything at all. They were just playing the same roles they played on social media and the consequences of playing an online game came as a devastating shock when they were confronted with the harsh facts. As Philip K. Dick has famously said, "Reality is that which when you stop believing in it, it doesn't go away."[19] Perhaps the most stunning example of what I am describing is Richard Barnett, the man who posted a photo of himself with his feet on House Speaker Nancy Pelosi's desk. After being charged with numerous crimes and jailed, Barnett lashed out in the courtroom and declared that the entire proceedings were "unfair" and "a load of crap." The court proceedings, jail, and his arrest are a bunch of crap since he firmly thinks that all he did was participate in some kind of role-playing game. Storming the US Capitol held no more reality for him and many others than professional wrestling or the jousting contests at a renaissance fair. The basis for his beliefs, for QAnon in general—and for just about everyone— that basis has been so thoroughly eroded and detached from the solid ground of lived life grounded in conjunctive relations that belief itself is lost. What is left is the mere replication of images and online performances of belief which can never withstand the test of anything beyond the closed ecosystems of belief manufactured by semiocapitalism and the digital engines of replication which keep the images moving with a patina of something new.

We can also take into account the relentless threats of civil war that became ubiquitous on the Internet and television throughout the Trump years. What emerged as threats of civil war turned out to be nothing more than an endless stream of images of men in paramilitary garb and rifles parading around for news cameras and for each other. The relentless stream of images, taken by the people performing these stunts and myriad others, filled television screens, Internet news outlets, and social media, and not one of the groups behind these images and threats materialized into anything other than performances. One may argue that the threat to kidnap the Governor of Michigan counts as a legitimate and lethal threat, but this is the exception that proves the rule. There have always been those on the fringe who have shown themselves willing to take things to lethal extremes. We can go back to Ruby Ridge and David Koresh, these are real. But the overwhelming majority of actors now are just that—actors. The people behind the plot to kidnap Gretchen Widmer were genuine exceptions.

These conditions are not exclusive to rightwing extremists and conspiracy theorists. Within seconds of a police shooting, the hashtags #BLM and #defundthepolice circulate around the globe at the speed of light. While a great many people are actively engaged in resistance protests to police brutality and systemic racism, there are also a vast number of people who feel as though they are actively engaging problems and issues like race, racism, and law enforcement abuse and are taking satisfaction from posting these hashtags and memes which signal their commitments and activism. Many of the people posting and sharing the hashtags and memes are doing nothing but reacting to online news, social media, and other instant images that pop up on their phones and recirculating meaningless modes of participation which in fact guarantee there is no actual participation with real events. We are not even engaging things through the voice of another. We are engaging a simulated environment in cyberspace which creates the illusion of interactive engagement that does nothing but satisfy AI bots who glean data from the systems and those who use them in the service of semiocapital which is itself the engine of everything that people claim to resist. The great reward to the user is the ability to espouse a firm belief that has the foundation of action to back up this belief when in fact all that is accomplished is the passive consumption of a simulacrum of belief and the empty gesture of action that requires nothing more than a tap on the screen of a smartphone.

Given that the entirety of the Q conspiracy and virtually everything else like it have all existed exclusively online, it is, at this stage, impossible to claim that these "beliefs" are beliefs. These ideas are circulated and exchanged in the same ways that every other online commodity is circulated and exchanged. Just as you are able to get on Amazon and buy a T-shirt with the logo of the Red Army Faction and declare your anarchist bona fides, so you can just as easily get on your smartphone and enact your fantasies of patriotism in the form of the Q conspiracy. You can also just as easily manifest your commitment to environmentalist causes by filling your shopping cart at Whole Foods with organic produce, and you can do this with an Amazon Prime account and pay for it all with your Aspiration card. What amounts to belief is nothing more or less than impenetrable and all-encompassing facts of semiocapital, and all that stands for belief are the commodities offered by the systems that reproduce and disseminate capital.

The ground on which anything that stands as belief is thoroughly eroded, and while people are actively doing things in the world, they are doing these things in the same way that they are boosting their favorite sports team or supporting the war with a sticker on their vehicle that says, "Support Our Troops." They are not playing a sport, and they are definitely not fighting a war. They are participating in a group activity that is an extension of their online presence and holds no more meaning than their online persona. Those who "stormed the Capitol" shared the entire event on their social media accounts in the same way they share photos of their dinners. The people who stormed the Capitol Building are in shock that they are being charged with crimes because nothing they do has anything to do with a fundamentally grounded reality. Their actions are a profound extension of the unreal reality that is the spectacle as the spectacle takes on the illusion of interactive dimensions which are the empty gestures of interpassivity. Actions carried into the world are extensions of fantastic and spectacular performances which are understood in the same terms as the meaningless gestures on the Internet which give rise to and guide these actions. These empty and futile gestures are the ruins and relics of all that is left of belief itself.

Notes

1. Will, George. "Shallow Look at the Mind of an Assassin."
2. DeLillo, Don. *Libra*. 58.
3. Douglas, Uscinski, Sutton, Cichocka, Nefes, Ang, and Deravi. "Understanding Conspiracy Theories." 7.
4. Bifo. *And: Phenomenology of the End*. 26.
5. Bifo. *And: Phenomenology of the End*. 26.
6. Bifo. *And: Phenomenology of the End*. 26.
7. Guattari, Felix. *The Three Ecologies*. 49–50.
8. Althusser, Louis. *Lenin and Philosophy and Other Essays*. 294.
9. Fisher, Mark. *Capitalist Realism*. 4.
10. Debord. *The Society of the Spectacle*. 12.
11. Debord. *The Society of the Spectacle*. 13.
12. Debord. *The Society of the Spectacle*. 13.
13. Debord. *The Society of the Spectacle*. 15. (My emphasis.)
14. Debord. *The Society of the Spectacle*. 16.
15. Debord. *The Society of the Spectacle*. 16.
16. Foucault, Michel. *The Order of Things*. 29.
17. Bifo. *And: Phenomenology of the End*. 260.
18. Moskalenko, Sophia, and Clark McCauley. "QAnon: Radical Opinion versus Radical Action." 142.
19. Dick, Philip K. *Valis*. 80.

"McScuse Me!"

As the spectacle has taken over the whole of social life to the extent
that individuals now understand their relations to the world,
each other, and themselves entirely through the mediation of
images, what once could function as an imaginary relation with
the real conditions of existence is now an imaginary relation
with distorted digitized images of images which individuals
consume in precisely the same ways that they consume any
other exchangeable commodity. As a result, what functions as
systems of knowledge and understanding have been subsumed
by systems of consumer capital. More, consumer capital unfolds
in the bourgeois sphere almost exclusively within the systems
of semiocapital: the forms of economic exchange in which
commodities are exchanged in the forms of digital signifiers.
Thus, the distortions that stand in for anything that may serve
as "real" are now thoroughly removed from living human
existence. Individuals now select bits of digital imagery that suit
already existing ways of understanding, and they misrecognize
this as the substance of belief. In this way, religion and faith
can take place in an amusement park in place of an active
investment in religion and belief. We can also be completely
relieved of all active living engagement with social, economic,
and even environmental issues by allowing our digital presence
to perform our engagement for us, and by using specific forms
of semiocapitalist exchange as the mediator between ourselves
and the world as it exists. The example of the Aspiration card
was a case in point. Individuals now derive their primary
sense of their most intimate self-identification as subjects from
within consumer capital. The social, cultural, and economic
conditions that make belief itself possible are now completely
determined and oriented with a regime of "truth" which is now
one in which individuals have been rendered as subjects who

must now dispense with veracity and truth in favor of a truth as exchange value. What is true is that which has value as a unit of consumer exchange. What one believes is a function of what one can purchase, and individual investments in truth are dispensed through external mechanisms of pseudo-actions in the form of consumption.

Under these conditions, Habermas's citizen-subject is supplanted by the contemporary citizen-consumer. Althusser's theory of ideology is rendered meaningless within a network of images of ideas that stand in for all material conditions, thus rendering any possibility of an imaginary relation as a purely fantastic relation that never corresponds to lived life. These conditions are exponentially accelerated within semiocapitalism as the machines of communication have taken precedence over all other forms of communication. Hardt and Negri explain that semiocapital reorganizes "communication" as it "not only expresses but also organizes ... the movement [of communication] by multiplying and structuring interconnections through networks."[1] These networks are what Bifo explains and describes as modes of connective communication which deny human modes of conjunctive communication. Under these conditions, the ways communications and knowledge find legitimation are no longer those defined by Habermas, Althusser, or any other existing systems of legitimation which underpin knowledge and belief. This form of legitimation "rests on nothing outside itself and is reproposed ceaselessly by developing its own language of self-validation."[2] Self-validation, then, becomes the measure by which individuals lay claim to core beliefs and their very sense of being a subject in society. To legitimize what now stands in for belief, we need only look to something like the Aspiration card as a mode of action which sustains our belief in protecting the environment. Again, anyone can buy a Red Army Faction T-shirt on Amazon to represent their belief in revolutionary politics. We can go to a faith-oriented theme park to have our faith in the Christian God played out before us through an interactive mechanical performance. Our rights as citizens are one and the same with our right to purchase consumer products. We can see these conditions fall into conflict as soon as we look at consumer culture in action.

There has been no end to reports of conflict surrounding demands that people wear masks to protect against the spread of COVID-19. Private businesses, of which restaurants and other service sector industries have been at the fore, have fought a relentless battle against individuals who believe they have the right to refuse to wear a mask to enter the premises. These are private businesses, not government offices and buildings, and to demand that someone wear a mask is completely within the rights of individual business owners. Some incidents over the issue of wearing masks have grown dangerously violent. The right-wing news industries and countless populist politicians have equated these demands that people wear masks with the abortion debate, that the demand that someone wear a mask on their face is a restriction over the physical body on an equal level as the regulation of women's bodies. This endless equivocation is bound up in the belief as a consumer choice problem, and I will return to this below. At this point, the very idea of regulating or interfering with an individual's right to freely consume now functions on the same terrain as individual sovereignty over the self and as a citizen of the nation.

Even in the absence of the mask mandates in businesses, there has been a steady increase in outrageous and even violent behavior in places like restaurants and cafes. Consumer desires are on an equal footing with civil rights. Angry and violent outbursts in restaurants, cafes, and bars are seen as acts of civil disobedience. A report in *The New York Times* summed the problem up by stating that "consumers had been seduced into the idea of the 'frictionless economy'—the notion that you could get whatever you wanted, the moment you wanted it."[3]

The problem of angry customers and an increase in incivility are attributable to many factors, but chief among them is the notion that individuals have come to view their rights as consumers as of a piece with their rights as citizens. The two subject positions have merged into the same thing. When someone does not get what they want, they view this as an affront to their civil rights. There is a popular short video that circulated a few years ago of a woman who addresses the people after being treated poorly at McDonald's. While the video was mistaken as real, it was in fact the work of a comedian named Libbie Higgins. The joke is revealing, though, in that Higgins' caricature of an American stereotype tropes on ideas that are quite serious. The woman in the video opens her monologue by saying she has announcement to make to "the people of America." Her ethos is as a person of the people who addresses "the People." Here, the people are the vast public who frequently go to McDonald's, people who know the routine, the language of the drive-through, the commercial jingles, and, most importantly, the special deals available at any given time. The People of America are McDonald's patrons. We recognize ourselves, we are "hailed" or interpellated as subjects by the *I'm Lovin' It* jingle. The jingle and the words pepper our everyday speech. We all know when we hear the familiar tune that this is the McDonald's tune, and we know what it means.

The main issue in the clip is that the woman is furious over her treatment at this particular McDonald's location. She ordered a McRib. When she was not offered the promised extra McRib with the purchase of the size she ordered, she reminds the person behind the counter. The counter person then insults her by telling her she does not look like she needs an extra sandwich. This is where we get the punchline of the clip in which the woman says, "McScuse me, bitch!" She goes on to explain the inherent problems in this situation, and at one point she says, with great emphasis, "This is against my civil rights!" It sounds absurd and it would be absurd if not for the fact that she is ideologically interpellated, as are the rest of us, as a citizen-consumer of and by McDonald's and the entire system of fast food, complete with its commercial systems of promises and promotions. She aligns her civil rights with her correct participation in the system of consumer capital, and we need to wonder why anyone would say she is wrong. This woman spoke the language of McDonald's correctly, she understood her right to the advertised special, and she was a fully valid paying customer. She had a right to get what she was promised and the fact that the person behind the counter fat-shamed her makes the entire transaction completely invalid. The joke works because it adheres to the actual conditions it purports to lampoon.

What is now recognized as internal and personal values are in fact the values instilled by the debt relation and that which equates consumption with civic participation. One of the most glaring examples came within the early weeks of the Coronavirus pandemic in the United States. There were massive protests and even violent resistance to any state and federal measures that would shutter businesses. Lieutenant Governor of Texas, Daniel Patrick, became a focal point in this resistance when he publicly declared that we should be willing to let elderly people die to save the economy. Patrick stated that a government-mandated shutdown "could end American life as he knows it, and that he is willing to risk death to protect the economy for his grandchildren."[4] Nearly 80% of the US economy is made up of service industries. What this boils down to is that Lieutenant Governor Patrick equated the shutdown of consumer capitalism with the end of the United States and the "American way of life." So deeply embroiled into the life of the citizen-consumer is the ability to shop and dine that these things are on an equal par with the American life itself.

Yet, the loss of those conditions which structured communication and ideology that found purchase in living human communication and lived material conditions have not fallen into a chaotic free-fall in which every individual freely chooses what stands in for reality. These conditions have been supplanted and replaced with a different set of social/cultural mechanisms which situate individuals within systems that determine how they can and must see themselves within the society of the spectacle and the forms of pseudo-belief that operate as citizenship and individual sovereignty. These mechanisms fall broadly under what Deleuze defined as "societies of control." Freed of the rigor of disciplinary society, the contemporary citizen-consumer is not quite as free as he or she may choose to believe. Rather, contemporary mechanisms of control are far more insidious:

> In the societies of control, on the other hand, what is important is no longer either a signature or a number, but a code: the code is a *password*, while on the other hand the disciplinary societies are regulated by *watchwords* (as much from the point of view of integration as from that of resistance). The numerical language of control is made of codes that mark access to information, reject it. We no longer find ourselves dealing with the mass/individual pair. Individuals have become "*dividuals*," and masses, samples, data, markets, or "*banks*." Perhaps it is money that expresses the distinction between the two societies best, since discipline always referred back to minted money that locks gold in as numerical standard, while control relates to floating rates of exchange, modulated according to a rate established by a set of standard currencies. The old monetary mole is the animal of the spaces of enclosure, but the serpent is that of the societies of control. We have passed from one animal to the other, from the mole to the serpent, in the system under which we live, but also in our manner of living and in our relations with others. The disciplinary man was a

discontinuous producer of energy, but the man of control is undulatory, in orbit, in a continuous network.[5]

The society of control is what lies behind phenomena like the consumer-citizen who cannot distinguish between the role of consumer and the role of a citizen-subject within a political/ social/cultural arrangement. Individuals do not simply become *"'dividuals,'* and masses, samples, data, markets, or *'banks.'"* They are formed into these modes via powerful machines of communication under semiocapital, and they are rendered subjects of societies of control most effectively by the debt relation mentioned above. It is the system of debt and finance that converts individuals into malleable and controllable subjects who internalize their own control as they come to view their role as debtors as a system of morality and ethics.

In addition to being one of the most extreme engines of interpassivity as in the example of the Aspiration card, the problem of the indebted man creates a set of social conditions of control which also gives rise of a mode of being in society that equates individual validity with the ways we are valued and controlled under the regimes of the debt relation. The debt relation fundamentally alters and reconfigures the locus of sovereignty at the levels of both the state and the individual. Since the 1970s, money has been increasingly dislodged from any standard of value other than itself. As the process of neoliberalization has transplanted the weight of responsibility for value from a public, state-centered site, to one in which this weight is redistributed throughout the private sector, money as standard of value has shifted to money as debt. Lazzarato explains that "(f)inance has appropriated most of the functions of bank money to such an extent that central bank policies are strongly determined by the financial sector's demand for liquidity. Bank money, money that exists mostly on a computer screen, is issued by private banks based on debt—a debt that becomes its intrinsic nature such that it is also called 'debt-money' or 'credit-money.'"[6] The result is that what we call money is in fact debt. There is no money that is not attached and substantiated by the debt relation, and all that passes for money is now founded upon the debt relation: "money itself is 'debt.'"[7] As a result, things like a national central bank now rely on the private financial sector as the source and foundation of all economic power. The state is no longer sovereign as it becomes beholden to and dependent upon the private financial sector, and "(t)he independence of the Central Bank with regard to the Treasury is, in reality, a mask for its dependence on the markets."[8] This plays out at the level of individuals in a similar fashion.

The forms of dependence created by the debt relation extend into the life of the individual and give rise to forms of biopower which will underpin the ways the contemporary citizen-consumer comes to understand the ways individuals form relationships with the self, each other, and the world. Since there is no money but debt money, that is to say that money itself is debt, there is no way to access the entirety of contemporary life except through the mechanisms of the debt relation. The risks of debt, under neoliberal policies of privatization, have been transferred from the public in the form of the state to individual private interests. As private entities, they have the power to determine how to assess and regulate risk. Under these conditions, the "collective insurance against risks (old age, illness, unemployment, etc.) have been systematically replaced by private insurance wherever possible."[9] This amounts to a massive and complete redistribution of risk and responsibility from collective agencies to private businesses and individuals. This redistribution operates as a form of freedom in which individuals are free to choose and take responsibility for their own lives and freely choose how they will manage their own lives. However, since the only way to access these freedoms is by assuming the debt relation, individuals must render themselves as valid within the terms and conditions of the debt relation as it is dictated by private financial systems. Individuals are not "expected to reimburse in actual money, but rather conduct, attitudes, ways of behaving, plans, subjective commitments, the time devoted to finding a job, the time used for conforming oneself to the criteria dictated by the market and business."[10] This mode of social control is defined explicitly by Foucault in *The Birth of Biopolitics* as the point at which "society appears as the consumer of conforming behavior, that is to say, according to the neo-liberal theory of consumption, society appears as the producer of conforming behavior with which it is satisfied in return for a certain investment."[11] In short, individuals are compelled to make good on their private responsibilities to their individual debt relation by adjusting their behavior, attitudes, ways of thinking, and forms of life to the conditions dictated by those private entities that grant or deny access to the debt relation. Individuals trade individual freedom for an illusion of freedom that is in fact a system which takes absolute control of life. To be a citizen-consumer, one must first be deemed valid within the debt relation as it is controlled and dictated by financial capital.

The source and foundation to subjectivity under this form of biopower within societies of control is such that the citizen-consumer finds its measure of validity and sovereignty from the degree to which it operates in accordance with the demands and dictates of the financial system of control mediated and dictated by the debt relation. Access to money means taking on the debt relation, and this means to be thoroughly and completely subjected to these mechanisms of control. At least one immediate result is that one's sovereignty as a citizen is indistinguishable from one's sovereignty as a valid and legitimate consumer. When the woman claims that McDonald's violated her civil rights by not offering her the extra McRib, she is acting in accordance with these conditions. When a customer is told to put a mask on their face in a private business, this is interpreted as an attack on the sovereignty of the individual citizen.

It is crucial to keep in mind that the individual who is subjected to and within the debt relation is simultaneously captured within the digital realm of consumer culture as it functions in twenty-first century technology. We do not simply go shopping and buy things. Contemporary consumer capital unfolds entirely within the digital realm. Even in-store purchases are linked to data acquisition algorithms that gather data on consumer patterns and behavior. Still, the overwhelming majority of consumer activity is done online, and a majority of this activity is with the use of smartphones and smart devices, this according to a consumer statistical tracker called *PaymentCloud*. All consumer activity uses algorithms to collect and analyze data to track individual and collective patterns, and these are not just spending patterns. These algorithms are designed to make online consumption as simple and free of friction as possible so as to render the presence of the online systems natural features of everyday life. Our society has become oriented by and towards these algorithms: "These interface-mediated processes are part of the so-called 'algorithm society,' in which the idea of machine learning encourages constant monitoring (through geolocation, the use of apps that require access to contact details, the use of online services and networks, city sensorization, etc.), which is described as a collateral effect and a necessary step for reaching the next level of comfort and efficiency."[12] Yet, the drive toward comfort and efficiency is more far-reaching as these systems become a feature of everyday life, so much so that the systems that employ these algorithms no longer refer to users as "users." The system is careful to use the term "people," and this way living people are "naturalized" (and neutralized) and the computational component is eliminated even as "they are subjected to surveillance that is programmed into the algorithms."[13] The final relevant point in this is that these systems do not simply collect data in order to optimize consumer choice. The algorithms and the systems they drive are actively modifying human behavior. The ease of use and friction-free experience is designed to render the system part of the ambient conditions of everyday life. As a result, users (people) begin to adopt the logic of the system itself. The goal of the algorithm is not to anticipate our behavior. Rather, the goal is to condition our behavior toward the logic of the interface and the algorithm. In short, "algorithms invite those who interact with them to adopt their own logic, and this often leads to standardization based on their own pre-defined objectives."[14] In these ways, connection completely subsumes conjunction; living human agency is replaced by digital patterns and drives; the citizen-consumer, whose individual freedom is nothing more than the freedom to choose "correct behavior" as it is defined by the debt relation, need never think about how to act and behave since the algorithm teaches them how to act and behave.

Just as spectacular conditions are accelerated and compounded by the digital realm, so the modes of capture and control are accelerated and compounded as the debt relation makes it possible for the citizen-consumer to find freedom the illusion of financial freedom and consumer choice as life itself is completely drawn into the mechanism of control, while willingly handing over the internal process of choice itself becomes conditioned and controlled by algorithms that teach us how to exchange being for having.

Notes

1. Hardt and Negri. *Empire*. 32.
2. Hardt and Negri. *Empire*. 33.
3. Lyall, Sarah. "A Nation on Hold Wants to Speak to the Manager."

4. Beckett, Lois. "Older people would rather die than let Covid-19 harm U.S. economy." The *Guardian* newspaper.
5. Deleuze. "Postscript on the Societies of Control."
6. Lazzarato, Maurizio. *The Making of the Indebted Man*. 97.
7. Lazzarato, Maurizio. *The Making of the Indebted Man*. 97.
8. Lazzarato, Maurizio. *The Making of the Indebted Man*. 98.
9. Lazzarato, Maurizio. *The Making of the Indebted Man*. 103.
10. Lazzarato, Maurizio. *The Making of the Indebted Man*. 104.
11. Foucault, Michel. *The Birth of Biopolitics*. 256.
12. Belsunces, Andreu. "The Commodification of Everyday Life."
13. Belsunces, Andreu. "The Commodification of Everyday Life."
14. Belsunces, Andreu. "The Commodification of Everyday Life."

The Violence of the Vacuous

One of the most important effects of these conditions is that subjectivity is manifested entirely as the image of subjectivity. Who we are, what we do in daily life, what we *believe* — none of this matters as much as the images of who we are, what we do, and what we believe. The process of applying for employment, for example, now depends entirely on an online profile. It would be redundant to list the online employment systems and apps that serve as mediators between individuals and potential employers. The most menial jobs now require an online application, and these demand an online profile. When individuals apply for employment, a digital image of these individuals is evaluated by algorithms and online systems far in advance of anything that could be construed as human-to-human contact. The point is that our living reality is mediated by our digital image. To be a valid participant, to function in the world in any meaningful way means to exist as an image, and this image is subjected to the same systems of evaluation as all other images of all other commodities. In short, our digital data becomes another level of spectacularity and abstraction. The full measure of subjectivity is reified as exchangeable data that is quantified and valuated. The existence of the citizen-consumer as subjected to the systems of control represented by the debt relation converts the whole of subjective being into an objectified, that is to say *reified*, object of exchange. Where Lukacs spoke of the reification of labor as commodity, his analysis was restricted to labor as it is captured within the mode of labor exploitation: "the objectification of their labour-power into something opposed to their total personality (a process already accomplished with the sale of that labour-power as a commodity) is now made into the permanent ineluctable reality of their daily life."[1] The subject here is objectified as a unit of exchange value within the confines of labor. Under our current conditions, in which one must objectify the totality of everyday life, the totality of the human is now a reified unit of exchange. Thus, what I am is my image of myself. My value is determined by my exchange value within the debt relation and my validity as a consumer. Finally, my sovereignty as an individual subject of civil society is now thoroughly overdetermined by my circulation within consumer capital as a commodity to be consumed. The sovereign subject is the subject as it is objectified—reified—as a unit of exchange, and this is total, no longer a feature of labor time, but life itself. The debt relation, the forms of life derived from and conditioned by the society of the spectacle, and the increasing dominance and control of algorithm society are all "controlled abstractions." No longer simply objects of industrial capital, our self-recognition as subjects is derived from a thoroughly internalized collection of systems of control whereby we can only understand "reality" in terms of how it measures up according to our own internal value. Being and thinking function in relation to systems of consumer value, and belief in the broadest sense is derived in relation to exchange value. Belief is exclusively substantiated within the logic of exchange.

Individuals must conform to the demands of the debt relation in every aspect of everyday life. This is how the debt relation exerts the biopolitical mechanisms of control. One must first demonstrate the ability to pay back the debt. To pay the debt, one needs to be not only employed but sufficiently employed. Anything that could jeopardize the basic conditions, breaking the law, speaking out on issues potential employers may find disagreeable, any kind of aberrant behavior such as drug or alcohol abuse, etc.—all of this permeates the fabric of everyday life and produces a subject of biopolitical control, of societies of control. What is more, individuals are not evaluated on these terms as individuals. They are evaluated in the form of data profiles like credit scores, employment histories, credit records, etc. In short, individuals adhere to societies of control through the mediation of the image of themselves. It is here that the spectacle permeates all levels and dimensions of human life, and it is here the societies of control completely determine the value of individual lives in the form of the image of individual lives, and it is at this stage that we see precisely what the Invisible Committee mean when they explain that this is the stage at which Empire penetrates the most intimate spheres of everyday life:

> Society's final moment of socialization, Empire, is thus also the moment when each person is called upon to relate to themselves *as value*, that is, according to the central mediation of a series of controlled abstractions. The Young-Girl would thus be the being that no longer has any intimacy with herself *except as value*, and whose every activity, in every detail, is directed to self-valorization. At each moment, she affirms herself as the *sovereign subject* of her own reification.[2]

As the citizen-subject comes to relate themselves as value, they emerge from the private sphere and come fully under the capture and control of the exchange of commodities as it is conditioned and overdetermined by the debt relation. No longer individual subjects, citizen-consumers are themselves individual images of commodities to be valued and validated by the same systems that value and validate every other commodity while they are under the complete control of biopower as it is expressed and mediated by the debt relation. The individual whose civil rights are a function of their ability to consume and their access to forms of consumption is a living commodity, a Young-Girl, in competition within the markets of consumer value, and the Young-Girl is fully legitimated not by their civil rights but by the financial legitimacy governed and controlled by financial access to the economic system. What the Young-Girl believes is the measure of the self in the realm of exchange value, and the Young-Girl is valid because the debt relation has validated her.

In evoking the figure of the Young-Girl, it is absolutely crucial that we be clear that the Young-Girl is neither young nor a girl. The Invisible Committee are clear on this from the outset: "(t)he Young-Girl is not a gendered concept," but "the *model citizen* since World War I."[3] The Young-Girl is the logical extension over all of life of the form of life that is the result of the complete colonization of everyday life by the spectacle. It begins in the 1920s when "capitalism realized that it could no longer maintain itself as the exploitation of human labor if it did not colonize everything that is *beyond* the strict sphere of production."[4] The emergence, or creation, of the Young-Girl comes out of the way consumer culture was able to extend the domestic sphere over all of life and render individuals in a suspended state of adolescence. Citing Stuart Ewen from *Captains of Consciousness*, the Invisible Committee explain that consumerist culture centered on youth and femininity as the primary sites of capture for the full emergence of consumer culture over all of life:

Young people, because adolescence is the period of time with none but a consumptive relation to society. Women, because it is the sphere of *reproduction*, over which they still reign, that must be colonized. Hypostasized Youth and Femininity, abstracted and recoded into *Youthitude* and *Femininitude*, find themselves raised to the rank of ideal regulators of the integration of the Imperial citizenry. The figure of the Young-Girl combines these two determinations into one immediate, spontaneous, and perfectly desirable whole.[5]

These two determinations align perfectly with what I have described as the penetration of the spectacle into the very being of individuals, the capture of individuals within societies of control in the form of the debt relation. The historical foundation of consumerism as it is situated within what we once called the public sphere was partially embedded in the evolution of the newspaper itself. Matthew Wills demonstrates that influence of what was once called the "Women's Page" has everything to do with the modern newspaper in America:

Before the Civil War, newspapers were partisan, party-sponsored sheets which aimed to rally voters—none of them female. In the later nineteenth century, newspapers became commodities, funded by advertisements, primarily, and subscriptions. By 1910, women were the center of advertising strategies. By the 1930s, "Mrs. Consumers" were believed to be key to the future success of the American economy.[6]

What were "Mrs. Consumers" if not the prototype of the Young-Girl? The reign of consumer logic over everyday life was achieved by extending the twin domains of the domestic sphere and the cognitive capacities of adolescence over all of life. Looking at Lt. Governor Patrick of Texas, what is he but the outspoken teenager from the crowd of teenagers, clambering about the rights of his "people" to continue doing just exactly as they please. The frictionless experience of the consumer, embedded into the habits, the DNA of everyday life, finds a champion in a "statesman" who loudly proclaims that some should die to sustain life as it is, and he wins over a huge percentage of the population because the mass of consumers already understand their rights as citizens to be their rights to consume while their validity as subjects within consumer capital is guaranteed by their valid status within the debt relation.

Individuals transformed into the figure of the Young-Girl participate in life via electronic media as patrons, as customers and as products. The image of the self that is valuated and validated as data finds its mode of equality and liberty as reified objects of exchange, and the value of the individual is determined by biopower rather than in the form of some presupposed value as a human. When we see people storming the Capitol Building in the name of freedom, what we are watching is a mob of angry patrons indistinguishable from those who rage at baristas and restaurant servers. They did not get their freedom in the same way they did not get their extra McRib. This is the rage of an infantilized people whose investment in political belief operates on the same terrain as their investment in their purchase power, who equate their validity as Homo economicus, Homo consumptor, and the indebted man with their role as citizen subjects engaged in rational critical debate. Within this phase of social/political life, individuals exist insofar as individuals have value, and since it is the individual who is the entrepreneur of their own lives, it falls to the individual to valorize themselves. What is more, to self-valorize means to *exist* as a spectacular image of yourself, and this image is regulated by the mechanisms of the society of control. This is the full manifestation of citizen-consumers in the form of the Young-Girl.

Things like ethical and moral conduct and the ground of belief are now conditioned by a culture of the algorithm and the image of the self that is validated by economic interests over human interests. What makes me an ethical person is not my actual conduct or what I truly believe. What makes me an ethical person is the fact that I have been fully validated by the debt relation as an individual who is qualified to participate in the debt relation that determines my place in society. If I have been validated according to my online profile, a profile that is primarily determined by data analysis based on my credit rating, employment history, and criminal background check, what I believe is necessarily true and what I believe is derived entirely from a spectacular representation of the world I live in. This spectacular representation is itself fully determined by algorithms that not only offer me images of the world, but also have been training me to consume these images as a passive receptor of data.

The world becomes less an ecosystem of thought and ideas and more of an enclosed terrarium of self-generating images that rely on the closed system of images for its existence. All information and knowledge are processed and legitimated by the systems of digital algorithms. To access information of any kind involves accessing these things through the online digital realm, and this is mediated by algorithms. None of these algorithmic interventions and mediations are disinterested. They process data according to assigned logics which determine things like relevance and importance. The legitimation of knowledge itself completely mediated by digital mechanisms:

> These algorithms, which I'll call public relevance algorithms, are—by the very same mathematical procedures—producing and certifying knowledge. The algorithmic assessment of information, then, represents a particular knowledge logic, one built on specific presumptions about what knowledge is and how one should identify its most relevant components. That we are now turning to algorithms to identify what we need to know is as momentous as having relied on credentialed experts, the scientific method, common sense, or the word of God.[7]

The production and certification of knowledge is the very process of legitimizing truth, ethics, morals, and belief. Since access to information is now entirely a function of online activity (even television is now a digital stream via the Internet), all information and all knowledge, all that can ever exist as knowledge and information is a priori conditioned by the mediation of algorithms. The other dimension to this is that individuals exist within the same system of legitimation. To be validated as a subject within the dual mediation of the spectacular existence and the debt relation necessarily means that self-validation is a projection of the self-image that is a reflection of economic validity. To be a subject is to exist as a Deleuzian "dividual" that is fully atomized within societies of control and consumerist spectacular existence. These conditions also give rise to the terrarium of existence. Unlike an ecosystem that is linked for its survival to all other ecosystems in an endless and reciprocal system of mutual life, the terrarium is closed and lives only according to the atomized system that provides only what is necessary for the finite collection of life that can exist in the closed system. It lives only to produce and reproduce itself, completely cut off from all other modes of life.

The emergence of the Young-Girl as a dominant mode of forms of life is also the point at which the spectacle has become integrated into the deepest reaches of life. No longer the mediating feature of reality and everyday life, individuals are now themselves spectacular representations of themselves to themselves. Subjectivity itself is now that mode of alienation and separation intrinsic to the society of the spectacle. Everything from an online profile for employment and banking to the performance of the self in the pseudo-public sphere of social media now renders individual lives as images of reified objects of exchange. The validity of one's life is measured according to the ways we are validated within the debt relation and the ways lives are validated according to "likes" on Facebook and Instagram. And the transfer of civic engagement to consumerist desire along with the validation of freedom in the form of economic freedom to participate in the most powerful mechanism of control necessarily produces a mass of infantilized dividuals who equate freedom with individual desire. Something as dangerous as white grievance can only become a matter of simple consumer choice in a world in which all things, no matter their cultural significance, and no matter the consequences of life and death, exist only as one among all other consumer choices. Andrew Culp observes that the digital realm operates as a "virtual subject," one that offers individuals the foundation for "everyday thinking."[8] The complementary mechanisms of the validation through the debt relation and the spectacular network of the digital and diffused spectacle function to provide the coordinates of morality, ethics, and knowledge while situating individuals in a purely fantastic relation with the world, one in which the virtual image of the self is prioritized over the living self: the Young-Girl, and one of the key features of the Young-Girl as the sovereign subject of her own reification, the Young-Girl "is a commodity that appears to desire its acquirer."[9] The dividual that emerges is one that desires, above all else, the validation of "the virtual subject" that grants the value and validation.

Not Economically Viable

A *New York Times* article from May 15, 2020, revealed the perils of working in retail and other service industries during the time of mask mandates. The mandate to wear a mask to prevent the spread of COVID-19 became so contentious that it bred violence across the country, and service industry workers have borne the brunt of this violence. With mandates that have no legal enforcement mechanisms, it was left to store clerks, servers, baristas, etc. to enforce mask mandates and policies, and then deal with refusals that often became physically violent. This same article details everything from insulting behavior to lethal attacks. People who refused to comply with mask mandates often cited their personal civil rights as justification. There has been a common feeling that the mask mandate has been a case of government over-reach, one that violates individual rights. This same *NYT* article describes a moment in which a customer was told to wear a mask in a *Trader Joe's* in California:

The customer, Genevieve Peters, who was recording the entire exchange, refused. "We are in America here," she said, "Land of the free." Then she turned her camera on other shoppers, who were less than amused: "Look at all of these sheep that are here, all wearing this mask that is actually dangerous for them."[10]

How different is this from the woman in the joke video who complained of her mistreatment at McDonald's over her McRib? Is this not the same sentiment only in a deadly serious context? This customer is not just taking a stand for her own personal liberty, she goes on to turn on others who she sees as "sheep" who buckle under the tyranny of the mask mandate. The context here is crucial. This customer is a fully valid paying consumer. She is a fully valid and legal subject as defined by the systems of financial validation that bestow upon her the legal right to spend her money in an open retail establishment. She is a free subject as defined by her ability to spend her money, and she is expressing this right by attempting to be a valid consumer. The store, *Trader Joe's*, has violated her civil rights. In this case, the consequences were minor. The woman finally left the store. In other cases, people fought for their legal subject status and their legal right to consume with deadly violence.

The 1993 film *Falling Down* offers a prescient look at the moments we see surrounding mask mandates and the service industry. Throughout the film, Michael Douglas's character, William Foster, later referred to by the name of "D-FENS" after the license plate on his car, wanders from one scene of middle-class consumer conflict after another, each marking an escalation in his rage and violence. Perhaps the most famous scene in the fast-food restaurant dramatizes the outraged consumer best. Foster becomes outraged and enraged when he is told he cannot order breakfast even though he arrived just minutes before the restaurant switched to the lunch menu. Outraged that his rights as a valid consumer are violated, he pulls out a machine gun and terrorizes the entire restaurant. This film has been thoroughly criticizèd for its portrayal of a white man on a rampage against contemporary "social ills and injustices" while it legitimizes this violent rampage in the form of something of an "everyman" for the frustrations of "the average male consciousness."[11] The backstory of the film is that Foster has been laid off from his job with a major defense contractor. He is a victim of the neoliberal corporate thinking that downsizes the average white man out of his job. His status as a delegitimized average white American man resonates perfectly with the white grievance of the current age, and his violent attacks on various modes of consumerism stand out as verging on an allegory of our current lashing out at the service industry. Much has been made of the violent outburst in Whammy Burger, the fictional burger joint in which Foster is refused breakfast because he is a few minutes late for the breakfast menu. This scene is telling since it hinges in part on the moment Foster asks the manager, Rick, if he has ever heard the expression, "The customer is always right"? But perhaps more revealing is the scene in which Foster enters a convenience store to get change for the phone. The store is run by a Korean man who behaves in a dismissive manner toward Foster and refuses to give out change unless he buys something. Foster decides to break a one-dollar bill on a Coca-Cola Classic, this, the very image of American consumer products, but becomes enraged when the price is too high and will not leave him change for the phone. Before wrestling a baseball bat away from the Korean man, who is simply trying to defend himself, Foster proceeds to smash the store to pieces after explaining that he is "standing up for my rights as a consumer."

The other crucial piece of this drama involves the conflation of two scenes. At one point Foster passes a man protesting in front of a bank because he had been refused a loan. The man, a black man, holds a sign that reads "NOT ECONOMICALLY

VIABLE." He repeats this line to passersby, and he is eventually arrested and taken away. As he is being put into a police car, he yells, "This is what happens when you are not economically viable." Later in the film, when Foster is almost completely defeated, he repeats this line when he says, "I'm obsolete. I am not economically viable." The machines of the societies of control in the form of the all-powerful debt relation have rejected these men, rendering them non-subjects, Homo sacer, if you will, alive but dead to the modes of existence that define our ability to exist in a world that legitimizes existence by our ability to be validated by financial capital and to express this valid status as a free consumer.

Far more than in 1993, the protagonist of *Falling Down* is the Everyman of the contemporary consumer citizen who has been thoroughly defined and validated by the societies of control. His entire life and livelihood have been derived from his precarious position in a contract position that is the epitome of neoliberal economic policies. His outrage and rage at everything he encounters is a response to one consumerist context after another in which his "rights" as a consumer are not properly honored and respected. Foster is the hero of our contemporary civil war against the white middle-class citizen-consumer whose very existence is defined within the debt relation as it has come to encompass the everyday life and the expression of individual life as it is verified in a society of the spectacle that penetrates the essence of everyday life. Foster is the dividual as it disintegrates in the face of systems that can only recognize living humans as expressions of specific forms of data. The problem at Whammy Burger has nothing to do with the customer or the manager, it is overridden by the programmed settings of the consumer machine that regulates an automated menu. And in the contemporary world, there is no recourse to negotiating prices. We have nothing like a medieval bread riot. To act against the laws of consumer culture is an act of war, and Foster knows it.

However, the convolutions and turnabouts presented by *Falling Down* all serve to present Foster as completely equal to the black man who is not economically viable and the Korean store owner who, with his broken English, is no longer an immigrant struggling for his piece of the American Dream but the perpetrator of American capitalist exploitation of middle-class Americans with his capricious price schemes. Our white male gets the opportunity to perform the greatest equivocation of all and comes to occupy the position as one who is racially marginalized and victimized the same as black people and immigrants. This is one reason the film has been so severely criticized. Carol J. Clover observes of *Falling Down*: "What distinguishes it from the average run-of-the-mill backlash fantasy is the demographic precision in which it identifies its protagonist not as any white male, but as an Average White Male, and the detail with which it defines that man's consciousness."[12] Clover's observation is that the protagonist here is the Everyman for all pissed off white men who are afraid their status of centrality within American culture might at some point be lost. Yet, this same observation is also why this film offers an almost ideal rendering of the contemporary Young-Girl who sees the violence of racism and modes of economic exploitation as another commodity among others and just one more role to play in the great spectacular realm that stands in for lived experience. If a white middle-class American man can take on the role of racial victim, one who is further victimized by predatory "foreigners," he is just as marginalized as any black man who is literally murdered by the police. The protagonist of *Falling Down* is not an Everyman; he is the thoroughly infantilized and domesticated Young-Girl that has been dislodged from the stable systems that bestowed its stability and status as "normal." Once removed from the mechanisms of control and once deprived of its ability to express freedom via the consumerist pathways that give spectacular life its meaning, the Young-Girl devolves into a violent tantrum that can escalate to real violence. Perhaps we can view the entirety of the nightmare surrounding Kyle Rittenhouse as the horrifying consequence of what happens when the Young-Girl mistakes its histrionic displays for the reality that remains even after it stops believing in it. After he murdered two people and after his subsequent acquittal, he can now operate as the soldier who fought and won the new civil war. Rittenhouse played out the violent fantasies that lie behind all the thwarted consumers and terrified white men who so desperately fear that they will be replaced.

Notes

1. Lukacs, Georg. *History and Class Consciousness*. 71.
2. Tiqqun. *Preliminary Materials for a Theory of the Young-Girl*. 18.
3. Tiqqun. *Preliminary Materials for a Theory of the Young-Girl*. 14–15.
4. Tiqqun. *Preliminary Materials for a Theory of the Young-Girl*. 15.
5. Tiqqun. *Preliminary Materials for a Theory of the Young-Girl*. 16.
6. Wills, Matthew. "The Unfolding of the Woman's Page."
7. Gillespie, Tarleton. "The Relevance of Algorithms."
8. Culp, Andrew. "Data, Media, Ethics: A Conversation with Andrew Culp."
9. Wark, McKenzie. *The Spectacle of Disintegration*. 200.
10. MacFarquhar, Neil. "Who's Enforcing Mask Rules? Often Retail Workers, and They're Getting Hurt."
11. Niedlich reads the film as a commentary on conservative criticisms of the breakdown of traditional values even as it revels in the violence of our modern everyman. Niedlich, Florian. "'No Time for the Innocent': Evil, Subversion and Social Criticism in Joel Schumacher's *Falling Down*, Bret Easton Ellis's *American Psycho* and Oliver Stone's *Natural*

Born Killers." AAA: Arbeiten Aus Anglistik Und Amerikanistik.
223. Clover's analysis directly addresses the problem of white male privilege as it emerges at the center of a culture of entitlement and complaint. The protagonist of *Falling Down* is a grotesque parody of the oppressed as he takes his vengeance on a world he has come view as aligned against the assumed rights of a middle-class white man.

12. Clover, Carol J. "'Falling Down' and the Culture of Complaint." 145.

Works Cited

Althusser, Louis. *Lenin and Philosophy and Other Essays*. Translated by Ben Brewster. New York: Monthly Review Press, 2001.

Beckett, Lois. "Older people would rather die than let Covid-19 harm US economy." https://www.theguardian.com/world/2020/mar/24/older-people-would-rather-die-than-let-covid-19-lockdown-harm-us-economy-texas-official-dan-patrick

Belsunces, Andreu. "The Commodification of Everyday Life." https://www.academia.edu/25422188/The_Commodification_of_Everyday_Life?email_work_card=view-paper

Berardi, Franco (Bifo). *After the Future*. Edited by Gary Genosko and Nicholas Thoburn. Edinburgh: AK Press, 2011.

— *And: Phenomenology of the End*. Cambridge: Semiotext(e), 2014.

Butler, Judith. *Gender Trouble*. Routledge, 2006.

Clover, Carol J. "'Falling Down' and the Culture of Complaint." *The Threepenny Review*, no. 54, 1993, pp. 32–33, http://www.jstor.org/stable/4384223 (Accessed 19 April 2022).

Culp, Andrew. "Data, Media, Ethics: A Conversation with Andrew Culp." https://www.academia.edu/41451040/Data_Media_Ethics_A_Conversation_with_Andrew_Culp?email_work_card=title)

Debord, Guy. *The Society of the Spectacle*. Translated by Donald Nicholson-Smith. New York: Zone Books, 1995.

Deleuze, Gilles. "Postscript on the Societies of Control." https://theanarchistlibrary.org/library/gilles-deleuze-postscript-on-the-societies-of-control

DeLillo, Don. *Libra*. New York: Viking Press, 1988.

Dick, Philip K. *Valis*. Boston: Mariner Books, 2011.

Douglas, K.M., Uscinski, J.E., Sutton, R.M., Cichocka, A., Nefes, T., Ang, C.S. and Deravi, F. "Understanding Conspiracy Theories." *Political Psychology*, 2019, 40: 3–35.

Fisher, Mark. *Capitalist Realism: Is There No Alternative?* London: Zero Books, 2013.

Foucault, Michel. *The Birth of Biopolitics: Lectures at the Collége de France, 1978-1979.* Translated by Graham Burchell. New York: Picador, 2008.

— "Of Other Spaces." *Architecture/Mouvement/Continuité.* October 1984; ("Des Espace Autres," March 1967, translated from the French by Jay Miskowiec).

— *The Order of Things: An Archaeology of the Human Sciences.* New York: Vintage Books, 1994.

Gallup. https://news.gallup.com/poll/248837/church-membership-down-sharply-past-two-decades.aspx (Accessed April 8, 2021).

Geer, John G. "The News Media and the Rise of Negativity in Presidential Campaigns." *PS: Political Science and Politics,* vol. 45, no. 3, 2012, pp. 422–427.

Gillespie, Tarleton. "The Relevance of Algorithms." In *Media Technologies,* edited by Tarleton Gillespie, Pablo Boczkowski, and Kirsten Foot. Cambridge, MA: MIT Press.

Gounari, Panayota. "Authoritarianism, Discourse and Social Media: Trump as the 'American Agitator.'" *Critical Theory and Authoritarian Populism,* edited by Jeremiah Morelock, vol. 9. London: University of Westminster Press, 2018, pp. 207–228.

Gramsci, Antonio. *The Antonio Gramsci Reader: Selected Writings, 1916-1935.* Edited by David Forgacs. New York: New York University Press, 2000.

Guattari, Felix. *The Three Ecologies.* Translated by Ian Pindar and Paul Sutton. London: The Athlone Press, 2000.

Habermas, Jurgen. *The Structural Transformation of the Public Sphere: An Inquiry into a Category of Bourgeois Society.* Translated by Thomas Burger. Cambridge: MIT Press, 1991.

Hardt, Michael and Antonio Negri. *Empire.* Cambridge: Harvard University Press, 2001.

Harvard Political Review. https://harvardpolitics.com/climate-change-responsibility/ (Accessed 8/11/21).

Hinton, Alexander. *It Can Happen Here: White Power and the Rising Threat of Genocide in the US*. New York: New York University Press, 2021.

Jain, Kalpana. "At a Popular Evangelical Tourist Site, the Ark Encounter, the Image of a 'Wrathful God' Appeals of Millions." *The Conversation*. https://theconversation.com/at-a-popular-evangelical-tourist-site-the-ark-encounter-the-image-of-a-wrathful-god-appeals-to-millions-179638#:~:text=The%20Ark%20Encounter%2C%20an%20evangelical,Noah's%20Ark%20from%20the%20Bible

Kellner, Douglas. "Preface: Guy Debord, Donald Trump, and the Politics of the Spectacle." *The Spectacle 2.0: Reading Debord in the Context of Digital Capitalism*, edited by Marco Briziarelli and Emiliana Armano, vol. 5. London: University of Westminster Press, 2017, pp. 1–14.

Kishan, Saijel. "Artificial Intelligence Used to Sniff Out Corporate Greenwashers." https://www.bloomberg.com/news/articles/2021-08-11/using-artificial-intelligence-used-to-find-corporate-greenwashers-green-insight (Accessed 8/22/21).

Laclau, Ernesto. *On Populist Reason*. New York: Verso, 2005.

Lazzarato, Maurizio. *The Making of the Indebted Man: An Essay on the Neoliberal Condition*. Translated by Joshua David Jordan. Los Angeles: Semiotext(e) Intervention Series 13, 2011.

Lukacs, Georg. *History and Class Consciousness*. Bibliotech Press, 2017.

Lyall, Sarah. "A Nation on Hold Wants to Speak to the Manager." *The New York Times*. January 1, 2022. https://www.nytimes.com/2022/01/01/business/customer-service-pandemic-rage.html (Accessed April 8, 2021).

Lyotard, Jean-Francois. *The Postmodern Condition: A Report on Knowledge*. Minneapolis: The University of Minnesota Press, 1984.

MacFarquhar, Neil. "Who's Enforcing Mask Rules? Often Retail Workers, and They're Getting Hurt." https://www.nytimes.com/2020/05/15/us/coronavirus-masks-violence.html

Makauskas, Nik. "Mapping the Contemporary Articulation of the Society of Control: Big-Data, 'Post-truth'-Disinformation and Network-Imperialism." https://www.academia.edu/2257984/The_Relevance_of_Algorithms?email_work_card=view-paper

Moskalenko, Sophia, and Clark McCauley. "QAnon: Radical Opinion versus Radical Action." *Perspectives on Terrorism*, vol. 15, no. 2, 2021, pp. 142–146.

Niedlich, Florian. "'No Time for the Innocent': Evil, Subversion and Social Criticism in Joel Schumacher's *Falling Down*, Bret Easton Ellis's *American Psycho* and Oliver Stone's *Natural Born Killers*." *AAA: Arbeiten Aus Anglistik Und Amerikanistik*, vol. 32, no. 2, 2007, pp. 221–40.

Pew Research Center. https://www.pewforum.org/2019/10/17/in-u-s-decline-of-christianity-continues-at-rapid-pace/ (Accessed April 8, 2021).

Pfaller, Robert. http://www.psychomedia.it/jep/number16/pfaller.htm (Accessed 6/1/2021).

Schumacher, Joel, Director. *Falling Down*. 1993.

Templeton, Michael. "Null Space and Null Existence Under the Spectacle." https://www.hamptonthink.org/read/null-space-and-null-existence-under-the-spectacle

Tiqqun. *Preliminary Materials for a Theory of the Young-Girl*. Translated by Ariana Reines. Cambridge: Semiotext(e), 2012.

— *Theory of the Bloom*. Translated by Robert Hurley. Creative Commons, 2012.

— *This is Not a Program*. Translated by Joshua David Jordan. Cambridge: Semiotext(e), 2011.

Wark, McKenzie. *The Spectacle of Disintegration: Situationist Passages out of the 20th Century*. New York: Verso, 2013.

Webb, Janette. "Climate Change and Society: The Chimera of Behaviour Change Technologies." *Sociology*, vol. 46, no. 1, 2012, pp. 109–125.

Will, George. "Shallow Look at the Mind of an Assassin." https://www.washingtonpost.com/archive/opinions/1988/09/22/shallow-look-at-the-mind-of-an-assassin/f8a4c3c6-8355-43c3-8a04-03d6588688e6/ (Accessed June 24, 2021).

Wills, Matthew. "The Unfolding of the Woman's Page." https://daily.jstor.org/the-unfolding-of-the-womans-page/

Zilber, Ariel. "Witches Now Outnumber Presbyterians in America as Number of Pagans Soar to 1.5 Million." https://www.dailymail.co.uk/news/article-6404733/Number-Americans-practice-witchcraft-estimated-high-1-5-MILLION.html (Accessed April 8, 2021).

Zizek, Slavoj. https://www.lacan.com/zizek-pompidou.htm. (Accessed 6/1/2021).

IFF
BOOKS

ACADEMIC AND SPECIALIST

Iff Books publishes non-fiction. It aims to work with authors and titles that augment our understanding of the human condition, society and civilisation, and the world or universe in which we live. If you have enjoyed this book, why not tell other readers by posting a review on your preferred book site.
Recent bestsellers from Iff Books are:

Why Materialism Is Baloney
How true skeptics know there is no death and fathom answers to life, the universe, and everything
Bernardo Kastrup
A hard-nosed, logical, and skeptic non-materialist metaphysics, according to which the body is in mind, not mind in the body.
Paperback: 978-1-78279-362-5 ebook: 978-1-78279-361-8

The Fall
Steve Taylor
The Fall discusses human achievement versus the issues of war, patriarchy and social inequality.
Paperback: 978-1-78535-804-3 ebook: 978-1-78535-805-0

Brief Peeks Beyond
Critical essays on metaphysics, neuroscience, free will, skepticism and culture
Bernardo Kastrup
An incisive, original, compelling alternative to current mainstream cultural views and assumptions.
Paperback: 978-1-78535-018-4 ebook: 978-1-78535-019-1

Framespotting
Changing how you look at things changes how
you see them
Laurence & Alison Matthews
A punchy, upbeat guide to framespotting. Spot deceptions and
hidden assumptions; swap growth for growing up. See and be free.
Paperback: 978-1-78279-689-3 ebook: 978-1-78279-822-4

Is There an Afterlife?
David Fontana
Is there an Afterlife? If so what is it like? How do Western ideas
of the afterlife compare with Eastern? David Fontana presents the
historical and contemporary evidence for survival of
physical death.
Paperback: 978-1-90381-690-5

Nothing Matters
a book about nothing
Ronald Green
Thinking about Nothing opens the world to everything by
illuminating new angles to old problems and stimulating new
ways of thinking.
Paperback: 978-1-84694-707-0 ebook: 978-1-78099-016-3

Panpsychism
The Philosophy of the Sensuous Cosmos
Peter Ells
Are free will and mind chimeras? This book, anti-materialistic but
respecting science, answers: No! Mind is foundational
to all existence.
Paperback: 978-1-84694-505-2 ebook: 978-1-78099-018-7

Punk Science
Inside the Mind of God
Manjir Samanta-Laughton
Many have experienced unexplainable phenomena; God, psychic
abilities, extraordinary healing and angelic encounters. Can
cutting-edge science actually explain phenomena
previously thought of as 'paranormal'?
Paperback: 978-1-90504-793-2

The Vagabond Spirit of Poetry
Edward Clarke
Spend time with the wisest poets of the modern age and of the
past, and let Edward Clarke remind you of the importance of
poetry in our industrialized world.
Paperback: 978-1-78279-370-0 ebook: 978-1-78279-369-4

Readers of ebooks can buy or view any of these bestsellers by
clicking on the live link in the title. Most titles are published in
paperback and as an ebook. Paperbacks are available in traditional
bookshops. Both print and ebook formats are available online.
Find more titles and sign up to our readers' newsletter at
www.collectiveinkbooks.com/non-fiction
Follow us on Facebook at
www.facebook.com/CINonFiction